Cont

Introduction

This collection of twenty-one short stories is suitable for students from the intermediate stage upwards. The extraordinarily high number of stories included in this selection results from their brevity: their length ranges from 185 to 1815 words. The first fifteen stories, in fact, have fewer than 800 words, which makes them ideal examination texts.

In terms of language and themes, the stories vary enormously. All texts, however, have in common that they are contemporary short stories. Most of them have been published since the end of the eighties and are consequently unknown as yet to teachers and students alike. Some stories include cultural references and may thus increase the student's insight into the country; all texts cover fundamental issues which are accessible and relevant for young readers.

Although all stories have been rated as masterpieces of their genre by dint of their publication in literary magazines and anthologies of new writing, their authors are mostly new talents yet to be recognized by the literary world. It is hardly surprising that many authors attended creative writing courses at American colleges and universities: the short story is known to be a popular art form in the United States. For this reason the dominance of young American writers in this collection is almost inevitable. We hope it has been made acceptable by the inclusion of a few writers from different English-speaking backgrounds.

Even though this collection of new short shorts can stand on its own, it is in a way incomplete without the students' workbook (*Creative Exercises*, cf. page 2). The authors' lack of literary reputation implies that almost nothing has been said about the stories yet by literary critics and this offers the teacher the opportunity to combine an established literary approach with new student-centred tasks from the workbook, which contains a wide selection of pre-reading and post-reading activities as well as of tasks for text comprehension and analysis. The underlying aim is to integrate language learning and literary analysis through learner-centred tasks which stimulate creative and emotional responses and encourage the use of the English language.

Fred Leebron

Water

She touches his hair by the river.

I am in our apartment, working. Her hand moves down his back.

I empty the trash and unclog the kitchen sink. His former girlfriends have turned into lesbians.

I take the key to his apartment, which he gave me so I could water his plants during the summer. He bends his kissing face to hers.

I walk over to his apartment, just two blocks away. Their legs dangle in the river.

I unlock the door and bolt it behind me. The room smells of feet and stale ashtrays. In the kitchen is a gas stove. I turn it on without lighting it.

Down by the river is a flock of geese, which they admire while holding hands. Soon he will take her back to his apartment. Soon they will lie there, readying cigarettes.

I relock the apartment and slip into the street. The air smells of autumn, burnt. In the sky, birds are leading each other south.

I know there is nothing left between us, that she looks at me each morning as if I were interrupting her life.

3 **trash** rubbish – **to unclog** to remove what is blocking s.th. up – 7 **to dangle** to hang loosely – 9 **to bolt** to fasten with a piece of metal (*verriegeln*) – 10 **stale** old and no longer fresh – **stove** oven, cooker – 12 **flock** group – 14 **to ready** to prepare for use – 18 **to interrupt** to break in on an activity, e.g. by talking

Paul Lisicky

Snapshot, Harvey Cedars: 1948

My mother touches her forehead, throwing her green eyes into shade. Her mouth is pink, her hair blond like wheat. She is tanned. She is the best-looking woman on the beach, only she will never recognize it. She wraps her long body in an aqua sarong and winces, believes her hips are a bell. Even now she is counting, waiting for the camera to flicker shut.

My father's arm weights down her shoulder. He is muscular, his stomach flat as a pan. He looks full ahead, pretending he is with my mother, but already he is in Florida, developing new cities, pumping dead mangrove full of sand. He sees himself building, building. He will be healthy. He will have good fortune. And years in the future, after his Army buddies will have grown soft and womanish, all his hard work will pay off: people will remember his name.

Their shoulders touch. Their pose says: this is how young couples are supposed to look – see, aren't we the lucky ones? But my mother's head is tilted. What is she looking at? Is she gazing at the tennis player by the outdoor shower, the one with the gentle hands, the one who will teach her to unlearn things? Or can she already hear the gun which my father will press into his forehead, twenty years away?

snapshot (*informal*) photograph taken without much preparation – 1 **forehead** ['fɒrɪd] part of the face above the eyes and below the hair – 2 **shade** shadow – **tanned** having a brown skin after spending a lot of time in the sun – 4 **to wrap s.th. in s.th. else** to put s.th. around s.th. else – **aqua sarong** [ˌækwə səˈrɒŋ] long piece of clothing worn around the waist, esp. by Malaysian men and women – **to wince** to make a sudden uncontrolled movement, e.g. with pain – 5 **hip** *Hüfte* – 6 **to flicker shut** to close with a light, quick movement – 10 **mangrove** ['--] a tropical tree that grows on coasts or river banks – 11 **fortune** ['fɔ:tʃu:n] luck – 12 **buddy** (*informal*) friend – 13 **to pay off** to be successful – 16 **to tilt** to move to one side – **to gaze** to look at s.th. for a long time

Gary Gildner

Fingers

When Ronald, Mr. Lacey's son, came home from the war, he showered, put on a pair of new jeans and a new T-shirt, found his old high-school baseball cap and pulled it down snug over his forehead, then went outside and shot baskets. He shot baskets for about two weeks. One day Mr. Lacey said, "What about that money you saved up? What are you going to do with it?" Ronald shot baskets for a while longer, then went downtown and bought an old Hudson Hornet. He spent five days driving the Hudson back and forth through town, stopping for a root beer when he got thirsty. On the sixth day, when a tire went flat, Ronald locked the car and put his thumb in the air. The next day in the Atkins Museum in Kansas City, he bought a dozen picture post-cards of Houdon's bust of Benjamin Franklin, because with that bald top and that long hair in back that fell to his shoulders, Franklin looked like the queerest duck he'd ever seen. Also Franklin seemed peeved about something. Then Ronald took a bus to New York City. The ride was nothing to crow about – and for maybe three hundred miles a man next to him wanted to describe losing his prostate gland. In New York, Ronald found a room a stone's throw from Yankee Stadium. He sent one of the Franklin cards to his father, saying only "Love, Ronald." Then he sat looking out the window. On the fire escape was a piece of red balloon that the wind was trying to blow away. Finally the wind succeeded and Ronald was tired. He took off his clothes, climbed into bed, and began to count the fingers on his shooting hand.

3 **snug** *here:* fitting closely – **forehead** ['fɒrɪd] part of the face above the eyes and below the hair – 4 **to shoot baskets** *(AE)* to throw the ball into the basket in basketball – 7 **Hudson Hornet** ['hɔːnɪt] name of a car – 9 **root beer** (*US*) sweet non-alcoholic drink – 10 **thumb** [θʌm] the short thick finger on your hand; you can use it to ask passing motorists for a ride – 12 **Houdon** [udõ] French artist – **bald** [ɔː] with little or no hair on the head – 14 **queer** strange – 15 **peeved** (*informal*) annoyed – 16 **to crow** [əʊ] **about s.th.** (*informal*) to speak proudly of s.th. – 17 **prostate gland** ['prɒsteɪt] *Prostata, Vorsteherdrüse* – 18 **Yankee Stadium** famous baseball stadium in New York

Lon Otto

Love Poems

He has written her a St. Valentine's Day love poem. It is very beautiful; it expresses, embodies a passionate, genuine emotion, emotion of a sort he hardly realized himself capable of, tenderness that is like the tenderness of a better man. At the same time, the imagery is hard, diamond clear, the form intricate yet unobtrusive. He says the poem out loud to himself over and over. He cannot believe it, it is so good. It is the best poem he has ever written.

He will mail it to her tonight. She will open it as soon as it arrives, cleverly timed, on St. Valentine's Day. She will be floored, she will be blown away by its beauty and passion. She will put it away with his other letters, loving him for it, as she loves him for his other letters. She will not show it to anyone, for she is a private person, which is one of the qualities he loves in her.

After he has mailed the poem to her, written out in his interesting hand, he types up a copy for his own files. He decides to send a copy to one of the more prestigious literary magazines, one into which he has not yet been admitted. He hesitates about the dedication, which could lead to embarrassment, among other things, with his wife. In the end he omits the dedication. In the end he decides to give a copy also to his wife. In the end he sends a copy also to a woman he knows in England, a poet who really understands his work. He writes out a copy for her, dedicated to her initials. It will reach her a few days late, she will think of him thinking of her a few days before St. Valentine's Day.

2 **to embody** *here*: to contain – **passionate** strong (of feelings) – 3 **capable of s.th.** ['keɪpəbl] able to do s.th. – **tenderness** *Zärtlichkeit* – 4 **diamond** ['daɪəmənd] – 5 **intricate** ['---] complicated – **unobtrusive** [ˌ--'--] not easily noticed – 9 **floored** *(informal)* completely surprised – 10 **to be blown away** to be deeply impressed – 15 **hand** *here*: handwriting – 16 **prestigious** [pre'stɪdʒəs] important, high-quality – 17 **to admit s.o.** *here*: to accept s.o. – **dedication** *Widmung* – 19 **to omit** (*formal*) to leave out

Richard Shelton

The Stones

I love to go out on summer nights and watch the stones grow. I think they grow better here in the desert, where it is warm and dry, than almost anywhere else. Or perhaps it is only that the young ones are more active here.

Young stones tend to move about more than their elders consider good for them. Most young stones have a secret desire which their parents had before them but have forgotten ages ago. And because this desire involves water, it is never mentioned. The older stones disapprove of water and say, "Water is a gadfly who never stays in one place long enough to learn anything." But the young stones try to work themselves into a position, slowly and without their elders noticing it, in which a sizable stream of water during a summer storm might catch them broadside and unknowing, so to speak, and push them along over a slope or down an arroyo. In spite of the danger this involves, they want to travel and see something of the world and settle in a new place, far from home, where they can raise their own dynasties away from the domination of their parents.

And although family ties are very strong among stones, many of the more daring young ones have succeeded, and they carry scars to prove to their children that they once went on a journey, helter-skelter and high water, and traveled perhaps fifteen feet, an incredible distance. As they grow older, they cease to brag about such clandestine adventures.

5 **to tend to do s.th.** to be likely to do s.th, to have a tendency to do s.th. – **one's elders** *(formal)* people older than oneself – 6 **desire** strong wish – 8 **to involve** to have to do with, to include – **to disapprove of** to dislike – 9 **gadfly** fly which bites cattle – 12 **sizable** *(AE)*/**sizeable** *(BE)* fairly large – 14 **slope** the side of a hill or valley – **arroyo** [ə'rɔɪəʊ] (*AE*) stream – 16 **to raise** *here*: to produce, to create – **dynasty** ['dɪnəstɪ] – 17 **domination** power, control – 19 **daring** full of courage – **scar** line or mark on the skin which is left after a wound has healed – 20 **helter-skelter** in great disorder and haste – 22 **to cease** [si:s] to stop – **to brag about s.th.** to speak about s.th. in an excessively proud way – **clandestine** [klæn'destɪn] (*formal*) secret

It is true that old stones get to be very conservative. They consider all movement either dangerous or downright sinful. They remain comfortable where they are and often get fat. Fatness, as a matter of fact, is a mark of distinction.

And on summer nights, after the young stones are asleep, the elders turn to a serious and frightening subject – the moon, which is always spoken of in whispers. "See how it glows and whips across the sky, always changing its shape," one says. And another says, "Feel how it pulls at us, urging us to follow." And a third whispers, "It is a stone gone mad."

2 **downright** (*informal*) completely – **sinful** against God's law – 4 **distinction** nobility, fame – 7 **to glow** to shine brightly – **to whip** *here*: to move quickly – 9 **to urge s.o. to do s.th.** to advise s.o. strongly to do s.th.

Grace Paley

Mother

One day I was listening to the AM radio. I heard a song: "Oh, I Long to See My Mother in the Doorway." By God! I said, I understand that song. I have often longed to see my mother in the doorway. As a matter of fact, she did stand frequently in various doorways looking at me. She stood one day, just so, at the front door, the darkness of the hallway behind her. It was New Year's Day. She said sadly, If you come home at 4 A.M. when you're seventeen, what time will you come home when you're twenty? She asked this question without humor or meanness. She had begun her worried preparations for death. She would not be present, she thought, when I was twenty. So she wondered.

Another time she stood in the doorway of my room. I had just issued a political manifesto attacking the family's position on the Soviet Union. She said, Go to sleep for godsakes, you damn fool, you and your Communist ideas. We saw them already, Papa and me, in 1905. We guessed it all.

At the door of the kitchen she said, You never finish your lunch. You run around senselessly. What will become of you?

Then she died.

Naturally for the rest of my life I longed to see her, not only in doorways, in a great number of places – in the dining room with my aunts, at the window looking up and down the block, in the country garden among zinnias and marigolds, in the living room with my father.

They sat in comfortable leather chairs. They were listening to Mozart. They looked at one another amazed. It seemed to them that they'd just come over on the boat. They'd just learned the first English words. It seemed to them that he had just proudly handed in a 100 per-

1 **to long to do s.th.** to want to do s.th. very much – 5 **hallway** *(esp. AE)* hall – 9 **meanness** intention to hurt – 12 **to issue** ['ɪʃu:] *here*: to publish – 13 **manifesto** written political statement – 14 **for godsakes** *informal expression used by s.o. who is angry* – 18 **senseless** without reason or purpose – 23 **zinnia** type of flower – **marigold** *Ringelblume* – 25 **amazed** astonished, very surprised

cent correct exam to the American anatomy professor. It seemed as though she'd just quit the shop for the kitchen.

I wish I could see her in the doorway of the living room.

She stood there a minute. Then she sat beside him. They owned an expensive record player. They were listening to Bach. She said to him, Talk to me a little. We don't talk so much anymore.

I'm tired, he said. Can't you see. I saw maybe thirty people today. All sick, all talk talk talk talk. Listen to the music, he said. I believe you once had perfect pitch. I'm tired, he said.

Then she died.

1 **anatomy** [ə'nætəmɪ] – 2 **to quit** to leave, to give up – 9 **to have perfect pitch** *das absolute Gehör haben*

Julia Alvarez

Snow

Our first year in New York we rented a small apartment with a Catholic school nearby, taught by the Sisters of Charity, hefty women in long black gowns and bonnets that made them look peculiar, like dolls in mourning. I liked them a lot, especially my grandmotherly fourth grade teacher, Sister Zoe. I had a lovely name, she said, and she had me teach the whole class how to pronounce it. *Yo-lan-da.* As the only immigrant in my class, I was put in a special seat in the first row by the window, apart from the other children so that Sister Zoe could tutor me without disturbing them. Slowly, she enunciated the new words I was to repeat: *laundromat, cornflakes, subway, snow.*

Soon I picked up enough English to understand holocaust was in the air. Sister Zoe explained to a wide-eyed classroom what was happening in Cuba. Russian missiles were being assembled, trained supposedly on New York City. President Kennedy, looking worried too, was on the television at home, explaining we might have to go to war against the Communists. At school, we had air-raid drills: an ominous bell would go off and we'd file into the hall, fall to the floor, cover our heads with our coats, and imagine our hair falling out, the bones in our arms going soft. At home, Mami and my sisters and I said a rosary for world peace. I heard new vocabulary: *nuclear bomb, radioactive fallout, bomb shelter.* Sister Zoe explained how it would happen. She

2 **charity** love and care for other people – **hefty** (*informal*) big and strong – 3 **gown** [aʊ] a long, formal dress – **bonnet** *Haube* – **peculiar** strange – 4 **mourning** [ɔ:] black clothes worn after s.o.'s death – 5 **Zoe** ['zəʊɪ] – 8 **to tutor** to teach – 9 **to disturb** *stören* – **to enunciate** [ɪ'nʌnsɪeɪt] *(formal)* to pronounce – 10 **laundromat** ['lɔ:ndrəmæt] (*US*) shop with washing-machines which people can use – 11 **holocaust** ['hɒləkɔ:st] great destruction in which many people are killed – 13 **missile** ['mɪsaɪl] explosive flying object that is used to destroy buildings and kill people – **to assemble** to put together – **to train s.th. on s.th.** to aim s.th. at s.th. – 16 **air-raid** attack by enemy aircraft – **ominous** hinting that s.th. bad is going to happen – 17 **to file** to walk one behind the other in a line – 19 **rosary** *Rosenkranz* – 21 **shelter** building that gives protection

drew a picture of a mushroom on the blackboard and dotted a flurry of chalkmarks for the dusty fallout that would kill us all.

The months grew cold, November, December. It was dark when I got up in the morning, frosty when I followed my breath to school. One morning as I sat at my desk daydreaming out the window, I saw dots in the air like the ones Sister Zoe had drawn – random at first, then lots and lots. I shrieked, “Bomb! Bomb!” Sister Zoe jerked around, her full black skirt ballooning as she hurried to my side. A few girls began to cry.

But then Sister Zoe’s shocked look faded. “Why, Yolanda dear, that’s snow!” She laughed. “Snow.”

“Snow,” I repeated. I looked out the window warily. All my life I had heard about the white crystals that fell out of American skies in the winter. From my desk I watched the fine powder dust the sidewalk and parked cars below. Each flake was different, Sister Zoe said, like a person, irreplaceable and beautiful.

1 **mushroom** (*Atom-*)*Pilz* – **to dot** to put dots (small round spots) on s.th.; *here*: to sprinkle, to put (chalkmarks) everywhere – **flurry** sudden heavy shower – 4 **breath** [e] air that comes out of the mouth – 6 **random** *here*: only few – 7 **to jerk** to move suddenly – 10 **to fade** to disappear slowly – 12 **wary** careful, looking for danger – 14 **to dust** *here*: to cover thickly – 15 **(snow)flake** thin piece (of snow)

Larry French

Mr. Mumsford

Bibs, the janitor, had never killed a man before. He'd raised rabbits as a boy and killed one now and then for supper. A quick blow to the back of the neck, and it was done. He was not a particularly intelligent man and was not suffering from guilt or any philosophical questions about what he was going to do. He had come to the small southern school as a janitor twenty-seven years ago. On his first day at school, he had worn a pair of old bib overalls and thus earned the nickname of Bibs. This was the reason he had come to kill the principal who was working late in his office down the hall. Earlier in the evening, Bibs had gone into the equipment room and picked out the largest baseball bat he could find. He then went and hid in a space between the green metal lockers that lined the hallways. At a little past ten the principal walked out of his office, locked it, and started down the hall. Bibs stepped out in front of him.

"Say, Bibs," asked the principal. "What are you doing here this time of night?"

Beads of sweat stood out on Bib's forehead, and he clenched the bat with both hands. He was six feet tall, very black, and towered over the principal.

"I come to kill you," said Bibs.

"But why? What have I ever done to you?"

"Just what you called me is why!" said Bibs. "Nobody in this school, including you, has ever bothered to learn my real name. Onliest person knows my real name is that woman signs my check, and even she

1 **janitor** person whose job is to look after a building – **to raise** *here*: to keep and feed – 2 **blow** [əʊ] a hard hit – 4 **guilt** feeling of having done s.th. wrong – 7 **bib overalls** *Latzhose* – **thus** (*formal*) therefore – **nickname** informal name used instead of s.o.'s real name – 8 **principal** (*AE*) headmaster – 10 **baseball bat** wooden stick used for hitting a baseball – 12 **to line s.th.** *here*: to form rows along s.th. – 17 **bead** small drop – **sweat** [e] water that comes through your skin when you are hot – **forehead** ['fɒrɪd] part of the face above the eyes and below the hair – 18 **to tower over s.o.** to be a lot taller than s.o. – 23 **not to bother to do s.th.** not to do s.th. because one thinks that it is not necessary – 24 **check** *(AE)* cheque *(BE)*

puts it in an envelope marked BIBS. The kids should learn my name in four years. Hell, I know more'n half of their names and where they live. This morning I stopped a couple of 'em and asked 'em did they know my real name, and they looked at me like I was crazy. That's why I come to kill you!"

The principal was a short man anyway, but now his shoulders slumped even further, and he looked sad and confused.

"Well," he said. "Well, what *is* your name?"

"Ralph Mumsford," said Bibs.

"Mumsford's a strange name for a black man to have," said the principal. "It's English, isn't it?"

"I don't know."

"You should look it up," said the principal. "You should go over to the school library and look it up. Say, lookee here, if I promise me and all my teachers call you by your real name from now on, will you not kill me?"

Bibs thought for a moment, seemed to waver, and then said, "Well, that seems fair. You do that, and I won't have to kill you."

The principal looked tired.

"You been working too many hours," said Bibs. "A Christian man ought to always eat the supper meal with his wife."

The principal sighed and said, "I do believe you're right, Mr. Mumsford. I do believe you have a point there." Then he turned and walked down the dark corridor toward the green exit sign leading out to the playground.

7 **to slump** to move downwards, to drop – 13 **to look s.th. up** to find s.th. out by looking in a book, e.g. a dictionary – 14 **lookee** (*informal*) look – 17 **to waver** to hesitate – 23 **to have a point** to be right

Ray Halliday

The Happiest Guy on the Train

I didn't see him at first but I heard him. I thought it was kids running around the station, playing a game, yelling EEE-ERR at one another, trying to keep each other from getting on the train in time. Then he jumped on real loud just as the doors were closing.

"EEE-ERR," he said. He was wringing his hands together, looking all over the train.

"Who's that?" someone on the train said.

"I don't know," someone else said.

The guy hopped up and down a little bit, then turned around and looked out the window. When the train started moving, he hopped up and down some more, said, "EEER-ERR," and looked out the window. He had his face so close to the window that it was getting all steamed up with his breath. I saw him try wiping the steam off with his hands, but I guess his hands were greasy, because the window kept getting messier and messier.

"He's just making it worse on himself," this older woman said.

The guy was moving his head back and forth real fast as things went by out the window. "YOR-OR," he said. He was wringing his hands. Then he turned around and looked back at everybody on the train. He scrunched his face up.

"Oh," this high-school girl said, "he's afraid. Afraid of the train." People on the train nodded in agreement.

"It's just a shame," a man in a sweatsuit said.

The guy would hop up and down and make noise, wring his hands together, look at things out the window when they came by and then whirl around like a dancer and look everybody on the train up and down, scrunching up his face and making noise.

2 **to yell** to shout – 5 **to wring (wrung, wrung) one's hands** *here*: to hold one's hands together and twist and turn them – 9 **to hop** to move in small jumps using only one foot – 13 **breath** [e] air that comes out of the mouth – **to wipe s.th off** to make s.th. disappear – 14 **greasy** oily – 20 **to scrunch s.th. up** *here*: to change s.th. into an unusual form – 23 **it is a shame** it is a pity

"Why is he looking at everybody?" the older woman asked.

"I don't know," said a man with a stroller. "But don't look right at him."

Everybody looked down. Everybody except for me. I felt like I wanted to help this guy. "He just wants you to look at him and smile," I said. "So he knows it's okay to be on the train." So I looked up, and the guy looked right at me with his face scrunched up, and I smiled. It's okay to be on the train, I smiled. It's safe. There are friends here.

"YEE-ERR," the guy said with gusto and started heading down the aisle.

"Nice going," the man with the sweatsuit said. "He's going to come over and fog your whole face up now."

"Oh, man," the high-school girl said.

"YOREE-ERR," the guy said, but went on past me. He ran down the aisle, making noise and jumping up and down. He looked out both sides of the train, wrung his hands together. He ran back to the door, jumped up and down.

"Wait a minute," the man with the sweatsuit said, "he's not afraid of the train. He loves the train."

"He thinks the train is great," the high-school girl said.

"It's a lot of fun for him," I said.

"He wants you to share his joy," the woman said.

"But don't look directly at him," the man with the stroller said.

And nobody did.

2 **stroller** (*AE*) small chair on wheels in which a baby or small child can be pushed around – 9 **gusto** energy and joy – **to head down s.th.** to move along s.th. – 10 **aisle** [aɪ] long narrow passageway that separates rows of seats

Richard Brautigan

Corporal

Once I had visions of being a general. This was in Tacoma during the early years of World War II when I was a child going to grade school. They had a huge paper drive that was brilliantly put together like a military career.

It was very exciting and went something like this: If you brought in fifty pounds of paper you became a private and seventy-five pounds of paper were worth a corporal's stripes and a hundred pounds to be a sergeant, then spiraling pounds of paper leading upward until finally you arrived at being a general.

I think it took a ton of paper to be a general or maybe it was only a thousand pounds. I can't remember the exact amount but in the beginning it seemed so simple to gather enough paper to be a general.

I started out by gathering all the loose paper that was lying innocently around the house. That added up to three or four pounds. I'll have to admit that I was a little disappointed. I don't know where I got the idea that the house was just filled with paper. I actually thought there was paper all over the place. It's an interesting surprise that paper can be deceptive.

I didn't let it throw me, though. I marshaled my energies and went out and started going door to door asking people if they had any newspapers or magazines lying around that could be donated to the paper drive, so that we could win the war and destroy evil forever.

An old woman listened patiently to my spiel and then she gave me a copy of *Life* magazine that she had just finished reading. She closed

1 **Tacoma** [-'--] American city in the State of Washington – 2 **grade school** (*AE*) primary school – 3 **paper drive** campaign for collecting paper – **to put together** to organize – 6 **private** (*noun*) soldier of the lowest rank (*Gefreiter*) – 8 **sergeant** ['sɑ:dʒənt] – **to spiral** [aɪə] to rise quickly – 12 **to gather** to collect – 13 **loose** [lu:s] *here*: lying around in several places – **innocent** *here*: harmless – 15 **to admit** to say that s.th. is true, often after hesitating – 18 **deceptive** leading to a wrong opinion – 19 **to throw s.o.** *(informal)* to confuse, upset or worry s.o. – **though** *here*: however – **to marshal** *here*: to collect – 21 **to donate** to give without asking for anything in return – 22 **evil** ['i:vl] (*noun*) everything that is very bad – 23 **spiel** [spi:l] speech that is repeated again and again

the door while I was still standing there staring dumbfoundedly at the magazine in my hands. The magazine was warm.

At the next house, there wasn't any paper, not even a used envelope, because another kid had already beaten me to it.

At the next house, nobody was home.

That's how it went for a week, door after door, house after house, block after block, until finally I got enough paper together to become a private.

I took my goddamn little private's stripe home in the absolute bottom of my pocket. There were already some paper officers, lieutenants and captains, on the block. I didn't even bother to have the stripe sewed on my coat. I just threw it in a drawer and covered it up with some socks.

I spent the next few days cynically looking for paper and lucked into a medium pile of *Collier's* from somebody's basement, which was enough to get my corporal's stripes that immediately joined my private's stripe under the socks.

The kids who wore the best clothes and had a lot of spending money and got to eat hot lunch every day were already generals. They had known where there were a lot of magazines and their parents had cars. They strutted military airs around the playground and on their way home from school.

Shortly after that, like the next day, I brought a halt to my glorious military career and entered into the disenchanted paper shadows of America where failure is a bounced check or a bad report card or a letter ending a love affair and all the words that hurt people when they read them.

1 **dumbfounded** [dʌm'faundɪd] totally surprised – 10 **lieutenant** [luː'tenənt] *(AE)*/[lef'tenənt] *(BE)* – 11 **not to bother to do s.th.** not to do s.th. because one thinks that it is not necessary – 12 **to sew** [əʊ], **sewed, sewn** or **sewed** to join pieces of cloth together with a needle and thread – **drawer** part of a desk or cupboard which can be pulled out and filled with things – 14 **cynical** ['sɪnɪkl] believing that all people are selfish and egoistic – 15 **Collier's** ['kɒlɪəz] American encyclopedia in 24 volumes – **basement** part of a building below the ground – 21 **to strut** to walk in a proud way, holding the head high – **airs** unnatural manners – 24 **disenchanted** disappointed – 25 **bounced** *here*: not accepted by the bank – **check** (*AE*) cheque *(BE)* – **report card** (*AE*) written report about a child's work at school, sent to its parents

Tom Hawkins

Wedding Night

I have worked at this bus station magazine stand since nineteen fifty three, waiting for the right girl to come along. When I took this job, the paint on that wall over there was new; it was a light green color then. The servicemen from the Korean War would stop and buy cigarettes, and I learned the insignia from the Army, Coast Guard, Navy, and Marines.

Once I was held up by a stocky white man in a brown jacket. Showed me the two teeth he had left in his head and the barrel of a little tape-wrapped automatic pointed at my heart. I gave him all the dough but never felt scared. Way I saw it, he was just like me, and I could die behind that counter and just walk away inside his skin, with a few dollars to spend. We were all one thing. So I handed him the money, feeling richer right away – three hundred twenty-three dollars – and let him get away before I called the cops.

I heard they never caught him, then I heard they caught him in another state – Utah I think – and then I heard they found him dead in an airport parking lot in Kansas. I don't know. He may be out there yet. He may be back. May hold me up tonight, or just shoot me dead, or both.

Anything can happen in the bus station. In the nineteen-sixties, we had what we called the hippies, young people in ragged get-ups. They used to sleep all over the furniture in sleeping bags, with packs and rolled-up tents.

4 **serviceman** member of the army, navy, etc. – **Korean** [kə'rɪən] – 5 **insignia** [ɪn'sɪgnɪə] (*pl.*) a badge or sign that one belongs to a certain organization – **Coast Guard** organization which watches the sea near a coast in order to help ships in danger or to fight smuggling – 6 **Marines** [mə'ri:nz] (*US*) special group of soldiers who are part of the American Navy – 7 **to hold s.o. up** to stop s.o. with a gun or knife in order to rob him – **stocky** short and strong – 8 **barrel** *here*: the long part of a gun – 9 **tape-wrapped** *mit Band umwickelt* – 10 **dough** [əʊ] (*slang*) money – **scared** frightened – 13 **right away** at once – 14 **cop** *(informal AE)* policeman – 16 **Utah** ['ju:tɑ:] – 17 **parking lot** (*AE*) car park – 21 **ragged** ['rægɪd] dirty and old – **get-up** (*informal*) unusual clothes – 22 **pack** *here*: bag, rucksack

That's when I began to think that the right girl might come along after all, some girl who'd grown tired of the long-haired boys, and tired of the road, and walk home with me and hold my hand, and curl up with me in my bed on my squeaky springs. I kept an eye out. One day I saw a young lady: she looked so long-tired and in need of a friend. I bought her a sandwich and coffee and a peanut-butter cup. I bought her some aspirin and a pint of milk, fingernail clippers and a souvenir shirt.

I told her I had a place where she could come to rest and stay, as long as she might want. I told her it wasn't fancy and wasn't but one room, but what was mine was hers. I knew it was clean. I'd cleaned it up the day before when I saw this girl hanging around.

She stroked my hair and said my heart was full of love. She said she had to sleep about twelve hours and then she'd go away. I took her home. She slumped down on the bed and cried – told me I was "so very kind." And then she slept like the dead. I lay down on the floor beside her, where I said I'd stay. In the middle of the night I woke up on fire, and the room was turning. I couldn't think. The air turned furry, where I crept up and slid in bed beside her, that girl still completely dressed. She breathed like the sea. I touched her skin, just her skin inside her clothes. She really never woke, just sighed and turned. In the morning when I woke up in the bed, she was gone.

I've worked here since nineteen fifty three, waiting for the right girl to come along. I guess she did. Some good marriages don't last long.

3 **to curl up** to lie comfortably with the arms and legs close to the body – 4 **squeaky** making a short, very high sound – **spring** *here*: a long round piece of metal which can be pressed down and will return to its original shape when you let go of it – 7 **pint** [paɪnt] 0.55 litre (*US*), 0.57 litre (*GB*) – **clippers** *(pl.)* tool for cutting nails or hair – 10 **fancy** (*informal*) very elegant – 13 **to stroke s.th.** to move a hand slowly over s.th. in a loving way – 15 **to slump down** to drop down heavily – 18 **on fire** *here*: hot – 19 **furry** ['fɜːrɪ] like fur *(Pelz)* – **where** *here*: when – **to creep, crept, crept** to move quietly and slowly – 20 **to breathe** [briːð] to take air into one's lungs and let it out again

Sheila Barry

Corners

Mildred and Jessie were elected to inspect Marie's remains before the public viewing. Mildred got to go because she was the oldest, and Jessie because she had come the farthest. The other siblings had gotten to pick out the casket and the dress their sister, Marie, would wear.

The undertaker, a former high-school classmate, showed them solemnly into the parlor. "I think you'll be pleased," he said as he lifted the casket lid and stepped back.

Jessie felt a familiar tug of pity for him, like the one she'd feel when she'd encounter him in school the day after she and her sisters had been making fun of him the night before.

"She looks wonderful, Tom," Mildred said. "You've done a good job. What do you think, Jessie?"

Jessie was crying, sobbing from the shock of seeing Marie dead and hearing Mildred and Tom discussing her body as if it were a float they were preparing for the Fourth of July parade.

Mildred put an arm around her. "There, there, Jessie," she soothed. "We keep forgetting you weren't here for Marie's last year. If you had been, you'd understand. None of us want Marie dead but none of us wanted her to go on suffering."

"She doesn't have to be smiling," Jessie sobbed. She turned on Tom. "Why did you put that silly smile on her face?" she demanded.

Tom's face panicked. "You don't like it?" he asked. His eyes sought Mildred's for confirmation.

1 **to inspect s.th.** to have a close look at s.th. – **remains** *here*: dead body – 2 **she got to go** she was allowed to go – 3 **siblings** brothers and sisters – **had gotten** (*AE*) had got – 4 **casket** (*AE*) box for a dead person – 5 **undertaker** person whose job it is to arrange funerals – **solemn** ['sɒləm] very serious – 6 **parlor** *(AE)*/**parlour** *(BE) here:* room where the coffin is – 8 **familiar** well-known – **tug** *here*: sudden, intense feeling – 9 **to encounter** [ɪn'kaʊntə] to meet – 13 **to sob** to cry in a noisy way – 14 **float** *here*: a large flat lorry on which a special show is carried in festival processions – 15 **Fourth of July** Independence Day, national holiday in the US – 16 **to soothe** [su:ð] to calm, to quieten – 22 **to seek, sought, sought** to look for – 23 **confirmation** agreement

"If Jessie doesn't like it," Mildred said, "then I guess you'd better change it."

"What do you mean, change it?" Jessie asked. "You can't change something like that!"

Tom reached over. He took the index finger of his right hand and tugged down on one corner of Marie's mouth which responded as if it were made of soft, malleable clay. Tom stuck his finger in the other corner of Marie's mouth and tugged down again. He stepped back. "How's that?" he asked. "Is that better?"

Mildred looked at Jessie expectantly.

"We can do anything you want with the mouth, Jessie," Tom said. He poised his index finger. "You just tell me what you want."

Jessie fled. She ran out, past the parking lot, around the corner to the high-school playing field.

Mildred found her there, sitting on the grass, hugging her knees. She sat down next to her. "Come on, kid," she said gently, "don't you think you're a little old for this?"

Jessie whipped her head around to look at Mildred. She thought she was ready, ready to tell Mildred what she really thought, how Mildred and Marie had been so close, how they had always left her out, even left her out of Marie's death. "Too old?" she demanded. "Too old?" she repeated to herself. That was the problem right there. None of them was any longer too young to die.

Mildred was smiling at her, tilting her head slightly to the side as if saying, Are you all right, are you ready to go on?

Jessie smiled back. Mildred nodded her head up and down, her smile growing with each movement. Then she poised her index finger in the air and waited.

Jessie laughed, quietly rocked back and forth, laughing until the tears rolled down her cheeks. She nodded and Mildred reached over with her index finger and pulled the corners of Jessie's mouth down. Jessie stuck out her index finger and pushed the corners of Mildred's mouth up. Down, up, down, up, they went, laughing then rolling on the ground until they could go back and tell Tom that Marie looked just fine.

6 **to tug** to pull quickly and strongly – **to respond** *here*: to react – 7 **malleable** ['mælɪəbl] (*formal*) easily changed into a new shape – **clay** *Lehm* – 12 **to poise** *here*: to hold in the air – 13 **to flee, fled, fled** to run away – **parking lot** (*AE*) car park – 15 **to hug** to hold close to one's body with one's arms – 24 **to tilt** to move to one side – **slightly** a bit – 29 **to rock back and forth** to move regularly backward and forward

Cynthia Forder

The Dragon

It was a porch-sitting night, so Bob and I moved out to the swing. Bob liked the swing, and sometimes he rocked it so hard that I felt seasick. We could see the city from the porch. At night, the lights made it look beautiful. The oil refineries looked like castles from a children's book. Some even breathed fire, as if dragons were inside.

Bob wasn't looking at the view. Things like that didn't interest him. He was talking about his relatives. He could be so boring. I didn't really hate him. He couldn't help it if he was boring and stupid.

My mother and Bob's mother were friends. That gave Bob a reason to come to see me every night. My mother liked Bob a lot. So I had to sit on the swing getting seasick. I watched the dragon in a refinery breathing fire. Bob was talking about his cousin Jimmy, who played bridge. Bob had a habit of repeating himself. I was glad when he came to the end. "Do you play bridge, Kay?"

"No," I said. I tried to make sure we had very little in common.

"How about going to the movies Saturday night?" he asked.

"I'm going to be busy then. Sorry."

"What are you doing?"

"I have some important poetry to write."

"You've been busy a lot lately, Kay."

I almost said, "Did you ever wonder why?" But I didn't.

Bob sighed. "I'm worried. It's April, and I haven't heard from a single college."

"Everything will work out," I said.

"You can say that because you're smart. College will be a breeze for you. But I want to be a lawyer, and it will be tough."

"You worry too much." I felt strange saying this. I felt law school *would* be tough for Bob. But I didn't want to be cruel.

dragon mythical animal which can fly and breathe fire *(Feuer speien)* – 1 **swing** *Schaukel* – 2 **to rock** to move regularly backward and forward – 7 **relative** member of the family, relation – 8 **he couldn't help it** he couldn't do anything about it – 24 **to work out** *here*: to have a good result – 25 **a breeze** (*slang; esp. AE*) something easily done – 26 **lawyer** *Rechtsanwalt*

He touched my shoulder. "You really don't like me, do you, Kay?"

"Bob, that's not a nice thing to say!" Suddenly, I felt guilty.

"But it's true. I'm not as stupid as you think."

"Have I ever said I didn't like you?" It bothered me that Bob might see through me.

"You didn't have to say it. I know."

"Bob, you know I think you're a great guy."

"I'm not a great guy. We both know I'm not. You think I'm stupid because you're smart. You think you're too good for me. I used to be happy here. Now I come because my mother makes me. You think I come here because I love you or something. Well, it isn't that. Not at all."

I felt wounded. I never thought Bob would see the truth.

"Kay, I'm going and I'm not coming back."

Suddenly, I was speaking. "Well, leave then! You *are* boring and dull. I only sit here because our mothers are friends."

I expected his eyes to look hurt. But they flashed with excitement. "I think that is the first time you've ever told me the truth. You're a phony, Kay. And that's worse than being stupid." He touched my shoulder again, gently. "I could like you, Kay. I really could. But the truth isn't important to you."

He smiled. To my horror, my eyes were filling with tears. The orange flame of the refinery blurred.

"Well, I'd better be going," Bob said. "I'm going to miss this swing."

I heard his car drive away. I got up and wiped my eyes on my sleeve. I went inside. My parents were watching television.

"Where did Bob go?" my mother asked.

"He … he had some poetry to write."

I stumbled into my room. From my bed, I watched the dragon's orange-and-red flame – until the colors melted and were washed away.

4 **to bother** [ɒ] to worry – 16 **dull** boring – 19 **phony** (*noun; informal*) s.o. who is not what he seems or pretends to be – 23 **to blur** to become unclear – 25 **sleeve** part of a piece of clothing that covers an arm – 29 **to stumble** to walk unsteadily, almost falling

Mary Dilworth

The Factory

I have always hated the factory. It has a gaunt steel frame like a skeleton. I've often imagined it without its red bricks, just an etching of black against a red sky.

Of course, I've never said anything about this to anyone. Especially to Eric. You see, he loves the factory. He would like to put up his sign in those flashing neon lights that the city firms can afford. He saw a rainbow once over a petrol station there. I think he would have sold almost anything to have one of those on his roof.

Every day he is up early. He sings in the shower and eats his breakfast quietly. He always reads the business section of the newspaper, then quarters it neatly.

His days are like that. In four parts.

The first is the morning, which I've mentioned. Then there's the day at the factory. That's in two: the morning and the afternoon.

He uses the telephone to tell me when it's time for lunch. Just two rings. That's his code. Then five minutes later he's at the door, letting himself in.

He reads at lunch, usually one of the classics. He didn't have much education.

In fact, that's why I met him. We worked at the same factory, ten miles out of town. It manufactured shoes and boots. I was the boss's secretary, and Eric worked the floor.

I'll always remember that first day. He was nervous, tried not to show it, but his hands shook. His hair was brown, his eyes were brown, and the factory overalls were brown. He almost faded into the background of brown leather shoes. Which was quite funny at the time.

1 **gaunt** [ɔ:] very thin – **frame** *here*: interior structure made of bars – 2 **brick** stone used for building houses – **etching** picture printed from a metal plate; *here:* outline – 11 **to quarter** to fold up twice, to a quarter of its size – **neat** tidy, careful – 22 **to work the floor** *(AE)* to have a job as an ordinary worker – 25 **to fade** *here*: to disappear

But I was describing his day. And he's not brown any more. Streaks of gray and a balding patch which he rakes over, spreading the hairs thinly across it. And he wears a suit. Usually gray, with a red handkerchief in the pocket. I suppose his eyes are still the same color, but I can't tell you. If you asked me, I just couldn't tell you. I did notice they were red tonight, which was unusual, but then the whole day was different. As though the four quarters came together and just rolled away.

I could draw the second half of his day with my eyes closed.

In the afternoon, he has a cup of tea in his office, then he works until six o'clock.

Two rings on the telephone mean he's coming home for dinner. He has a good appetite and enjoys his food.

In the evening he likes quiet. He always says that after such a busy day at the factory, he needs to sit and think. Which he does, with his eyes closed, his elbow on the chair, and his thumb and one finger pressed against his forehead. Or sometimes he just sits and stares into space.

Eric always goes to bed early. He feels fresh then for the next day.

But now the next day won't come. It won't be Eric's day, and his eyes are red. I've never seen him cry before.

I said this day was different. It's night now, and soon the dawn will come. In the night, the sky was red. A brilliant red. That was beautiful. Black against red. Like a devil with horns or the final crashing chords of a great concerto.

I loved it. Black skeleton of steel in a fiery night. Of course the fire brigade came. I didn't call them. It was beautiful just watching the sky burning. I don't think I will ever forget it. Eric was asleep.

They came to tell us as soon as they arrived. Eric knew straight away it was all over.

I love the night. Sometimes I stay up for hours, savoring it. The stars and that great arc of sky. The immense pattern, the changing moods of wind.

1 **streak** [i:] long stripe – 2 **gray** *(AE)* grey *(BE)* – **balding** beginning to lose the hair on the head – **patch** spot – **to rake over** to cover – 15 **elbow** the part of the arm connecting the upper and lower half – **thumb** [θʌm] the short thick finger that is set apart from the other four – 16 **forehead** ['fɒrɪd] the part of the face above the eyes and below the hair – 24 **chord** [k] *Akkord* – **concerto** [kən'tʃeətəʊ] piece of music for a solo instrument and an orchestra – 28 **straight away** at once – 30 **to savor** *(AE)*/**savour** *(BE)* to enjoy – 31 **arc** part of a circle, curve – **immense** very large – **pattern** regularly repeated form (*Muster*)

Tonight it was special. It was different. And I feel very tired. But happy. An exhilarated feeling, a prickling right down my spine.

Nobody knows how the fire started. Accidental, they say. It happens all the time.

2 **exhilarated** [ɪɡˈzɪləreɪtɪd] very happy and excited – **spine** row of bones down s.o.'s back that supports the body – 3 **accidental** not intended

Larry Fondation

Deportation at Breakfast

The signs on the windows lured me inside. For a dollar I could get two eggs, toast, and potatoes. The place looked better than most – family-run and clean. The signs were hand-lettered and neat. The paper had yellowed some, but the black letters remained bold. A green-and-white awning was perched over the door, where the name "Clara's" was stenciled.

Inside, the place had an appealing and old-fashioned look. The air smelled fresh and homey, not greasy. The menu was printed on a chalkboard. It was short and to the point. It listed the kinds of toast you could choose from. One entry was erased from the middle of the list. By deduction, I figured it was rye. I didn't want rye toast anyway.

Because I was alone, I sat at the counter, leaving the empty tables free for other customers that might come in. At the time, business was quiet. Only two tables were occupied, and I was alone at the counter. But it was still early – not yet seven-thirty.

Behind the counter was a short man with dark black hair, a mustache, and a youthful beard, one that never grew much past stubble. He was dressed immaculately, all in chef's white – pants, shirt, and apron, but no hat. He had a thick accent. The name "Javier" was stitched on his shirt.

I ordered coffee, and asked for a minute to choose between the breakfast special for a dollar and the cheese omelette for $1.59. I selected the omelette.

1 **to lure** [lʊə] to attract – 3 **neat** carefully done – 4 **bold** *here*: strongly marked – 5 **awning** *Markise* – **to perch s.th.** to place s.th. (usu. in a high position) – 6 **to stencil** to print – 7 **appealing** attractive – 8 **homey** (*informal AE*) pleasant, like home – **greasy** oily – 9 **to the point** giving only the information needed – 10 **entry** piece of information in a list – **to erase** to wipe out – 11 **to figure** (*informal, esp. AE*) to think, to guess – **rye** *Roggen* – 16 **mustache** ['mʌstæʃ] *(AE)*/**moustache** [mə'stɑːʃ] *(BE)* hair that grows on a man's upper lip – 17 **beard** [ɪə] hair that grows on a man's face – **stubble** very short hairs which can be seen on a man's face if he has not shaved recently – 18 **immaculate** perfect – **chef** [ʃef] (chief) cook in a restaurant – 19 **apron** piece of clothing worn over the front of the clothes, e.g. when cooking

The coffee was hot, strong, and fresh. I spread my newspaper on the counter and sipped at the mug as Javier went to the grill to cook my meal.

The eggs were spread out on the griddle, the bread plunged inside the toaster, when the authorities came in. They grabbed Javier quickly and without a word, forcing his hands behind his back. He, too, said nothing. He did not resist, and they shoved him out the door and into their waiting car.

On the grill, my eggs bubbled. I looked around for another employee – maybe out back somewhere, or in the washroom. I leaned over the counter and called for someone. No one answered. I looked behind me toward the tables. Two elderly men sat at one; two elderly women at the other. The two women were talking. The men were reading the paper. They seemed not to have noticed Javier's exit.

I could smell my eggs starting to burn. I wasn't quite sure what to do about it. I thought about Javier and stared at my eggs. After some hesitation, I got up from my red swivel stool and went behind the counter. I grabbed a spare apron, then picked up the spatula and turned my eggs. My toast had popped up, but it was not browned, so I put it down again. While I was cooking, the two elderly women came to the counter and asked to pay. I asked what they had had. They seemed surprised that I didn't remember. I checked the prices on the chalkboard and rang up their order. They paid slowly, fishing through large purses, and went out, leaving me a dollar tip. I took my eggs off the grill and slid them onto a clean plate. My toast had come up. I buttered it and put it on my plate beside my eggs. I put the plate at my spot at the counter, right next to my newspaper.

As I began to come back from behind the counter to my stool, six new customers came through the door. "Can we pull some tables together?" they asked. "We're all one party." I told them yes. Then they ordered six coffees, two decaffeinated.

2 **to sip** to drink, taking only a little at a time – **mug** a large cup with a handle – 4 **griddle** round flat piece of metal used for cooking – **to plunge** *here*: to put or place quickly – 5 **the authorities** *here*: the police – 7 **to resist** to fight against s.th. – **to shove** [ʌ] to push in a rough way – 10 **washroom** *(AE)* toilet – 17 **swivel stool** a seat that turns – 18 **spatula** ['spætjʊlə] kitchen tool with a wide flat blade – 23 **to ring up an order** to record and add up the prices on a cash register – 24 **tip** money given in addition to the official price – 31 **decaffeinated** [dɪ'kæfɪneɪtɪd]

I thought of telling them I didn't work there. But perhaps they were hungry. I poured their coffee. Their order was simple: six breakfast specials, all with scrambled eggs and wheat toast. I got busy at the grill.

Then the elderly men came to pay. More new customers began arriving. By eight-thirty, I had my hands full. With this kind of business, I couldn't understand why Javier hadn't hired a waitress. Maybe I'd take out a help-wanted ad in the paper tomorrow. I had never been in the restaurant business. There was no way I could run this place alone.

2 **to pour s.th.** [ɔ:] to fill a cup with s.th. – 3 **scrambled eggs** *Rühreier* – 7 **ad** (*informal*) advertisement

Ed Edmo

After Celilo

I'm not sure what it was that caused my going. Maybe youthful exuberance. I'd like to think it was the quest for knowledge and creativity. Lightning was my guide, and the moon was my protector as I stood by the road, sticking my thumb out to the world. It was the spring of 1964, when all the glories of high school football were over and there was only the dull future facing me. As I looked to the Columbia River, I remembered the many times I had gone there. The river was a welcome friend that never had to be called in for supper.

Celilo Falls attracted white tourists. Tourists in baseball caps, straw hats, pith helmets. Some were bald-headed. Tourists came to the falls to watch Indians fishing off of scaffolds. Tourists with sunglasses hanging from their sunburnt necks; their knobby knees bulging from beneath Bermuda shorts. They handed us silver quarters to pose with their children and their grandchildren. I liked to get next to a little white girl. If she was afraid, I'd move closer to her, and when she would get tears welling in her eyes, I'd reach out and grab her and giggle. You know, being next to a real Indian is really a frightening experience! The river was calming. I'd watch the soothing current and see the sun reflect off the silver waves.

In 1957, the government built The Dalles Dam and flooded us Indians out of our traditional fishing places. We didn't want to be flooded out, but they called it progress. I remember that they held

Celilo [səˈliːləʊ] – 1 **exuberance** [ɪɡˈzjuːbərəns] excitement, enthusiasm – 2 **quest** search – 3 **lightning** flashes of light during thunderstorms – 4 **to stick out a thumb** [θʌm] to ask passing cars for a ride – 6 **dull** uninteresting – 10 **pith helmet** large hat worn in the tropics to protect the head from the sun – **bald-headed** [bɔːld] with little or no hair on the head – 11 **scaffold** [ˈskæfəʊld] platform to stand on – 12 **knobby** *(AE)*/**knobbly** *(BE) knubbelig* – **to bulge** to stick out – 13 **quarter** (*US*) 25-cent coin – 16 **to well** to start to flow – **to grab** to take hold of – 17 **to giggle** [ɡ] to laugh quickly in a nervous way – 18 **to calm** to become quiet – **to soothe** [suːð] to make less excited, to quieten – 20 **Dalles** [dælz] – **to flood** [ʌ] **s.o. out of a place** to force s.o. to leave a place by covering it with water meetings in people's houses. Then we Indians would talk about our future and wonder what would happen to us. It was a hard time.

My father had seen the plans at The Dalles Chamber of Commerce and he tried to warn the people at Celilo. But the people only teased him and called him an ol' Chinaman because my father didn't wear braids like the other Indian men of the village. When the engineers began leveling the earth to make a new right-of-way for the Union Pacific Railroad, the Indians of the village saw that the government meant to do as they had planned. Many remembered that when Bonneville Dam was built in the 1930s, the Herman Creek Indians were forced to move but not compensated for any of their fisheries or their homes.

My father organized the Indians at Celilo Village to meet on a regular basis. We didn't want the government just to move us out and not compensate us for any of the fishing or our houses. My father wrote to Senator Neuberger of Oregon, who introduced a bill in Congress to have the government pay us for our fisheries and buy us new houses. At the time we were negotiating the amount of payment, the chief's son said, "You should pay us fifty dollars for every board in our drying sheds, because this is our way of life." The government man got angry and told us Indians that we should accept their "fair" offer, and that if we didn't, he would go to the judge at Wasco County and have our land condemned and bulldoze everything without paying us anything.

When the workmen finished surveying at the end of the day, some of us boys would pull out the stakes from the ground, fill the holes, and make a small fire out of the stakes. Others would climb the cliffs and shoot BB guns at the big dump trucks as they hauled dirt. We would laugh when a driver stopped his truck. In our own small way, we tried to stop the dam.

3 **Chamber of Commerce** ['kɒmɜːs] *Handelskammer* – 4 **to tease** to make fun of, to laugh at – 6 **braid** [eɪ] (*esp. AE*) long hair which has been twisted and tied – 7 **to level** to make flat – **right-of-way** (*noun*) *here*: main line – 16 **bill** first version of a new law to be discussed in Congress – 18 **to negotiate** [nɪ'ɡəʊʃɪeɪt] to discuss in order to come to an agreement – 22 **judge** *Richter* – 23 **to condemn** *(AE) here*: to take away by authority for a public purpose – 24 **to survey** [sə'veɪ] to measure and to make a map of an area of land – 25 **stake** piece of wood pushed into the ground – 26 **cliff** steep rock usu. on the coast – 27 **BB gun** (*AE*) children's gun – **dump truck** open-backed truck which can be tipped to empty *(Kipper)* – **to haul** [ɔː] to carry away

Finally, when we were moved out, we had to burn our house. I had to choose what to take and what to leave to get burned up. Just as Dad started the fire, I ran back into the house to get my bedside stand. It was an old commode. Later I was to get it refinished and it became an antique. We watched with mixed happiness and sadness as the old house went up in flames. We were to get a new house across the river.

We moved into an all-white community – Wishram, Washington. After a year of fighting, my brother and I were accepted into school. One time a little white girl got mad at me for some reason. She spit on me and told me to go back to where I came from. I couldn't go back because there was a freeway where my house used to stand. I couldn't understand why she said that.

I grew up in tough times. I learned how to escape into books and I knew the library. I was not hurt by the characters in the books. I could pick and choose from a world that accepted me and didn't put me down because I was an Indian or came from a poor village.

It was a bright sunset as I stood on the north side of the Columbia River and a blue car stopped.

"How far you goin'?" a young man asked.

"Portland," I said hopefully.

"Get in," he said.

He handed me a cigarette. The car ride was filled with country and western music and chitchat. We crossed the Hood River Bridge and drove west. He said that he was only going as far as Cascade Locks. I was glad for the ride. He dropped me off at the freeway exit.

"Good luck," he exclaimed.

"Thanks, man!" I replied.

The sun had set and it was almost dark. I began to get scared. A cop might be looking for a runaway from a small town.

Headlights shone on me as a car pulled over. I saw it was a pickup. I got to the side. I peered in and a tall black man sat behind the steering wheel.

"Get in, kid," he commanded.

4 **commode** [kəˈməʊd] – 9 **mad** *here*: angry – **to spit, spat, spat** (*also esp. AE* **to spit, spit, spit**) *spucken* – 15 **to put s.o. down** *(informal)* to make s.o. feel ashamed – 24 **chitchat** (*informal*) talk about things that are not very important – 29 **scared** frightened – **cop** *(informal AE)* policeman – 31 **to pull over** *here*: to move over to one side of the road – **pickup** small truck with low sides that can be easily loaded – 32 **to peer** to look very attentively

I hesitated, but he asked wearily, “Do you want a ride or not?”

I got in and we made small talk until we got to Portland. He drove me to the east end of the Burnside Bridge, where the transients and homeless stayed, and dropped me off.

“Walk across the bridge, kid, an’ you’ll find your people.” He said it matter-of-factly.

I thanked him and began walking across that bridge.

1 **weary** [ɪə] *(lit.)* tired – 3 **transient** ['trænzɪənt] (*formal*) s.o. who stays in a place for only a short time – 6 **matter-of-factly** showing no emotion

Spencer Holst

On Hope

The monkey leaped on the man's shoulder.

The man shuddered for he knew who it was. He knew exactly which monkey of the ten thousand that roam about on the Rock of Gibraltar, tame and free as pigeons, walking around in the parks and streets.

It was a demon monkey.

It was the one he'd trained to bring him necklaces, who brought him pearls, garnets, and amber from moonlit bedrooms in the big hotels – stolen from women sunk in snoring.

The monkey dangled before his eyes the largest diamond in the world.

The whole thing began several days previously when all on Gibraltar went into an uproar. The Rock of Gibraltar was visited by royalty, by the queen mother, and the princess. A battleship brought them and their entourage, and with them the famous necklace, the largest stone of which was the *Diamond of Hope*, which the princess was to wear at some great state occasion. (There's a curse on the necklace, you know, and misfortune had followed it, and come to whomever possessed it until it became part of the British crown jewels in the middle of the nineteenth century.)

On the very first night the royal party was in, the monkey returned to his gypsy master with the necklace. The necklace, of course, was valueless. It couldn't possibly be sold. Gibraltar would be swarming with police searching for it.

1 **to leap** to jump – 2 **to shudder** to shake uncontrollably for a moment – 3 **to roam** [əʊ] to wander – **Gibraltar** [dʒɪ'brɔ:ltə] – 4 **tame** not wild, trained to live with people – **pigeon** *Taube* – 6 **demon** ['di:mən] evil spirit – 7 **necklace** ['neklɪs] string of jewels worn around the neck – 8 **garnet** a red jewel (*Granat*) – **amber** *Bernstein* – 9 **to snore** to make noises when sleeping – 10 **to dangle** to swing – 13 **uproar** noise and shouting made by angry or excited people – 15 **entourage** [ɒntʊ'rɑ:ʒ] all the people who surround and follow an important person – 18 **misfortune** [mɪs'fɔ:tʃu:n] bad luck – 21 **party** *here*: group of people – 22 **gypsy** [dʒ] *Zigeuner* – 23 **valueless** worthless

The gypsy was annoyed with the monkey, irritated at its genius, and terrified of being caught by the police with the gems; and besides, although he had no particular regard for the government – (being a gypsy) he liked the idea of “the princess” and wouldn’t dream of stealing her necklace. So he quickly wrapped it up and addressed the package to her and dropped it in an ordinary mailbox. He enclosed a note to her saying something like, “You really ought to guard this more carefully.”

The next night the monkey returned again with the necklace.

This time his note implored her to have the police guard the necklace more carefully, and he even gave them advice. He advised them to place the necklace in the center of a cage.

(For a monkey, of course, couldn’t get into a locked cage.)

Then the third night, when this story begins, the monkey again brought the gypsy the necklace, and fell at the gypsy’s feet, dead. Shot. Very probably the monkey had been fatally wounded by a guard as he was escaping.

The gypsy shuddered at the diamond, and was not surprised at the death of his friend.

The first two times it had been like some freak occurrence, like a weird accident – to unexpectedly discover oneself in possession of part of the British crown jewels! But now …

When he received the gems for the third time the whole thing was plunged into meaning. It no longer seemed like an accident. He had been given the necklace. Fate was at work. Now, the necklace was his.

He put it in his pocket.

It never occurred to him (being a gypsy) to doubt the reality of the curse which accompanied the diamond, and he accepted his fate with the stone. Quietly and secretly he buried the animal.

1 **irritated** angry, impatient – **genius** ['dʒi:njəs] – 2 **terrified** extremely frightened – **gem** [dʒ] jewel or stone that is used in jewellery – 3 **regard** *here*: respect – 5 **to wrap s.th. up** to fold a piece of paper around s.th. – 7 **to guard** [gɑ:d] to watch and protect – 10 **to implore** to beg – 16 **fatal** deadly – 20 **freak occurrence** [ə'kʌrəns] strange event – 21 **weird** [wɪəd] very strange, unnatural – **accident** *here*: s.th. that happens unexpectedly, without being planned – 24 **to be plunged into meaning** to suddenly become meaningful – 25 **fate** power that is believed to control everything that happens – 27 **it never occurred to him** the idea never came to his mind – 28 **to accompany** *here*: to be connected with

And as he thought about it he was actually a little pleased that he, a gypsy, had been singled out by fate to take the curse off the princess, and the English throne.

He walked down to the shore of the Mediterranean and took off his clothes, and – having nothing in which to put the necklace, he put it on – dove in, and swam.

There was a full moon and the sea was perfectly calm.

Just off Gibraltar there's a very deep place in the Mediterranean. It's called the Gibraltar Trench. Only a mile from shore the sea is a mile deep.

The gypsy was a very good swimmer.

He swam out a mile, over this spot, took the necklace off and dropped it.

At that moment a smile lit his face as he imagined the thousands of Sherlock Holmeses searching for it for the next fifty years.

The man lazily began to swim back toward shore, and the necklace fell down into the depths.

They each had a mile to go – the man had a mile to swim, and the gems had a mile to fall.

The necklace fell much faster than the gypsy swam.

It fell straight down until it got about a hundred feet from the bottom, where it came to rest on the dorsal fin of a shark.

The shark had been sleeping, but the necklace woke it, and it turned round and around wondering what was happening. It decided to go up to investigate.

The shark swam upward even faster than the necklace had fallen.

Meanwhile the man still lazily swam toward the huge "rock," now ablaze as never before with the royal festivities, with a million electric light bulbs – and he thought of the curse. The stone would never bring its misfortune to anyone ever again; it was finished forever, its power over man extinguished for good, buried beneath a mile of water.

Then he looked over his shoulder and saw the necklace floating a foot above the water, moving slowly past him.

4 **the Mediterranean** [ˌmedɪtə'reɪnjən] the sea between southern Europe and North Africa – 6 **to dive, dived** (*AE* **dove**), **dived** to jump head first into water – 22 **dorsal fin** *Rückenflosse* – **shark** *Hai* – 25 **to investigate** to try to find out more about s.th. – 28 **ablaze** shining brightly – 29 **bulb** *Glühbirne* – 31 **to extinguish** *here*: to destroy – **for good** forever – 32 **to float** *here*: to move slowly and gently

(The gypsy did not see the shark's fin, he only saw the necklace glittering in the moonlight, as if floating in the air, not coming toward him, but moving past him, now receding into the distance.)

The man immediately realized that one of two things was true. Obviously, either he was witnessing a miracle (and the whole thing smacked of the miraculous), or he was having a hallucination.

He decided to find out.

Was it a miracle? or, was it a delusion?

He began to shout and wave his arms and splash, and he began to swim after the necklace.

And sure enough the necklace stopped and after a moment began to move toward the man.

The man is swimming toward the necklace. The necklace is moving toward the man.

That is where the story ends.

However, I can't help noticing, at this moment, that at first glance it seems inevitable – you know, that the shark will devour the man.

But I do not believe that result is as inevitable as it seems at first glance; that is, I believe there are several reasons, so to speak, for hope.

1. I do not think a shark has ever been approached like this before, that is, by a man wondering whether the shark is a miraculous manifestation, or whether it is merely a figment of his own imagination. Such a man would smell different.

2. The man is a gypsy animal trainer.

3. The shark is now in possession of the necklace.

3 **to recede into the distance** to move slowly away – 5 **to witness** to see – **miracle** wonder – 6 **to smack of s.th.** to make you think of s.th. – **miraculous** [mɪ'rækjʊləs] – 8 **delusion** false belief, illusion – 9 **to splash** to make water fly into the air – 16 **I can't help noticing** it is impossible for me not to notice – **glance** look, sight – 17 **inevitable** impossible to avoid, certain to happen – **to devour** [dɪ'vaʊə] to eat quickly and hungrily – 21 **to approach** to come near – 22 **a miraculous manifestation** a wonder – 23 **figment** product

Ray Bradbury

I See You Never

The soft knock came at the kitchen door, and when Mrs. O'Brian opened it, there on the back porch were her best tenant, Mr. Ramirez, and two police officers, one on each side of him. Mr. Ramirez just stood there, walled in and small.

"Why, Mr. Ramirez!" said Mrs. O'Brian.

Mr. Ramirez was overcome. He did not seem to have words to explain.

He had arrived at Mrs. O'Brian's rooming house more than two years earlier and had lived there ever since. He had come by bus from Mexico City to San Diego and had then gone up to Los Angeles. There he had found the clean little room, with glossy blue linoleum, and pictures and calendars on the flowered walls, and Mrs. O'Brian as the strict but kindly landlady. During the war he had worked at the airplane factory and made parts for the planes that flew off somewhere, and even now, after the war, he still held his job. From the first he had made big money. He saved some of it, and he got drunk only once a week – a privilege that, to Mrs. O'Brian's way of thinking, every good workingman deserved, unquestioned and unreprimanded.

Inside Mrs. O'Brian's kitchen, pies were baking in the oven. Soon the pies would come out with complexions like Mr. Ramirez' – brown and shiny and crisp, with slits in them for the air almost like the slits of Mr. Ramirez' dark eyes. The kitchen smelled good. The policemen leaned forward, lured by the odor. Mr. Ramirez gazed at his feet, as if they had carried him into all this trouble.

"What happened, Mr. Ramirez?" asked Mrs. O'Brian.

2 **tenant** person who rents a room, flat, etc. – 6 **overcome** *here:* unable to speak because of emotion – 8 **rooming house** (*AE*) building that is divided into rooms or flats which people rent to live in – 11 **glossy** shining brightly – 13 **landlady** woman who owns a rented building – 18 **to deserve** [z] to have a right to – **unreprimanded** [ˌʌnreprɪˈmɑːndɪd] without being criticized – 19 **pie** *Pastete* – 20 **complexion** skin colour – 21 **crisp** fresh, hard and dry (*knusprig*) – 23 **to lure** to attract – **odor** (*AE*)/**odour** (*BE*)) smell – **to gaze** to look for a long time

Behind Mrs. O'Brian, as he lifted his eyes, Mr. Ramirez saw the long table laid with clean white linen and set with a platter, cool, shining glasses, a water pitcher with ice cubes floating inside it, a bowl of fresh potato salad and one of bananas and oranges, cubed and sugared. At this table sat Mrs. O'Brian's children – her three grown sons, eating and conversing, and her two younger daughters, who were staring at the policemen as they ate.

"I have been here thirty months," said Mr. Ramirez quietly, looking at Mrs. O'Brian's plump hands.

"That's six months too long," said one policeman. "He only had a temporary visa. We've just got around to looking for him."

Soon after Mr. Ramirez had arrived he bought a radio for his little room; evenings, he turned it up very loud and enjoyed it. And he bought a wrist watch and enjoyed that too. And on many nights he had walked silent streets and seen the bright clothes in the windows and bought some of them, and he had seen the jewels and bought some of them for his few lady friends. And he had gone to picture shows five nights a week for a while. Then, also, he had ridden the streetcars – all night some nights – smelling the electricity, his dark eyes moving over the advertisements, feeling the wheels rumble under him, watching the little sleeping houses and big hotels slip by. Besides that, he had gone to large restaurants, where he had eaten many-course dinners, and to the opera and the theater. And he had bought a car, which later, when he forgot to pay for it, the dealer had driven off angrily from in front of the rooming house.

"So here I am," said Mr. Ramirez now, "to tell you I must give up my room, Mrs. O'Brian. I come to get my baggage and clothes and go with these men."

"Back to Mexico?"

"Yes. To Lagos. That is a little town north of Mexico City."

"I'm sorry, Mr. Ramirez."

2 **linen** ['lɪnɪn] things made of cloth that are used in the house (*here*: tablecloth) – **platter** large, flat plate used for serving food – 3 **pitcher** (*AE*) *Krug* – **cube** *Würfel* – 6 **to converse** *(formal)* to talk – 9 **plump** nicely rounded – 11 **temporary** ['tempərərɪ] limited in time – 14 **wrist watch** watch worn between the hand and the lower part of the arm – 17 **picture** *here*: film – 19 **streetcar** *(AE)* sort of bus on rails used in cities (*BE:* tram) – 22 **many-course dinners** dinners consisting of many different parts

"I'm packed", said Mr. Ramirez hoarsely, blinking his dark eyes rapidly and moving his hands helplessly before him. The policemen did not touch him. There was no necessity for that.

"Here is the key, Mrs. O'Brian," Mr. Ramirez said. "I have my bag already."

Mrs. O'Brian, for the first time, noticed a suitcase standing behind him on the porch.

Mr. Ramirez looked in again at the huge kitchen, at the bright silver cutlery and the young people eating and the shining waxed floor. He turned and looked for a long moment at the apartment house next door, rising up three stories, high and beautiful. He looked at the balconies and fire escapes and back-porch stairs, at the lines of laundry snapping in the wind.

"You've been a good tenant," said Mrs. O'Brian.

"Thank you, thank you, Mrs. O'Brian," he said softly. He closed his eyes.

Mrs. O'Brian stood holding the door half open. One of her sons, behind her, said that her dinner was getting cold, but she shook her head at him and turned back to Mr. Ramirez. She remembered a visit she had once made to some Mexican border towns – the hot days, the endless crickets leaping and falling or lying dead and brittle like the small cigars in the shopwindows, and the canals taking river water out to the farms, the dirt roads, the scorched landscape. She remembered the silent towns, the warm beer, the hot, thick foods each day. She remembered the slow, dragging horses and the parched jack rabbits on the road. She remembered the iron mountains and the dusty valleys and the ocean beaches that spread hundreds of miles with no sound but the waves – no cars, no buildings, nothing.

"I'm sure sorry, Mr. Ramirez," she said.

"I don't want to go back, Mrs. O'Brian," he said weakly. "I like it here, I want to stay here. I've worked, I've got money. I look all right, don't I? And I don't want to go back!"

1 **I'm packed** I have packed – **hoarse** [hɔːs] speaking in a rough and unclear voice – 6 **suitcase** flat container used for carrying clothes etc. when travelling – 9 **cutlery** knives, forks and spoons – **waxed** [æ] *here:* polished – 11 **story** *(AE)*/**storey** *(BE)* floor of a building *(Stockwerk)* – 12 **fire escape** stairs or ladder to be used in case of fire – **laundry** washing – 21 **cricket** *Grille* – **to leap** to jump – **brittle** hard but easily broken – 23 **scorched** burnt, dried out by heat – 24 **thick** *here:* heavy – 25 **to drag** *here*: to move very slowly and with difficulty – **parched** dried out by heat – **jack rabbit** a large North American rabbit with fairly long ears (*Eselhase*)

"I'm sorry, Mr. Ramirez," she said. "I wish there was something I could do."

"Mrs. O'Brian!" he cried suddenly, tears rolling out from under his eyelids. He reached out his hands and took her hand fervently, shaking it, wringing it, holding to it. "Mrs. O'Brian, I see you never, I see you never!"

The policemen smiled at this, but Mr. Ramirez did not notice it, and they stopped smiling very soon.

"Goodbye, Mrs. O'Brian. You have been good to me. Oh, goodbye Mrs. O'Brian. I see you never!"

The policemen waited for Mr. Ramirez to turn, pick up his suitcase, and walk away. Then they followed him, tipping their caps to Mrs. O'Brian. She watched them go down the porch steps. Then she shut the door quietly and went slowly back to her chair at the table. She pulled the chair out and sat down. She picked up the shining knife and fork and started once more upon her steak.

"Hurry up, Mom," said one of the sons. "It'll be cold."

Mrs. O'Brian took one bite and chewed on it for a long, slow time; then she stared at the closed door. She laid down her knife and fork.

"What's wrong, Ma?" asked her son.

"I just realized," said Mrs. O'Brian – she put her hand to her face – "I'll never see Mr. Ramirez again."

4 **fervent** showing deep feeling

Krishnan Varma

The Grass-Eaters

For some time several years ago I was tutor to a spherical boy (now a spherical youth). One day his ovoid father, Ramaniklal Misrilal, asked me where I lived. I told him.

Misrilal looked exceedingly distressed. "A pipe, Ajit Babu? Did you say – a *pipe*, Ajit Babu?"

His cuboid wife was near to tears. "A *pipe*, Ajit Babu? How can you live in a pipe?"

It was true: at that time I was living in a pipe with my wife, Swapna. It was long and three or four feet across. With a piece of sack cloth hung at either end, we had found it far more comfortable than any of our previous homes.

The first was a footpath of Chittaranjan Avenue. We had just arrived in Calcutta from East Bengal where Hindus and Muslims were killing one another. The footpath was so crowded with residents, refugees like us and locals, that if you got up at night to relieve yourself you could not be sure of finding your place again. One cold morning I woke to find that the woman beside me was not Swapna at all but a bag of bones instead. And about fifty or sixty or seventy years old. I had one leg over her too. I paid bitterly for my mistake. The woman very nearly scratched out my eyes. Then came Swapna, fangs bared, claws out ... I survived, but minus one ear. Next came the woman's husband, a hill of a man, whirling a tree over his head, roaring. That was my impression, anyway. I fled.

Later in the day Swapna and I moved into an abandoned-looking freight wagon at the railway terminus. A whole wagon to ourselves –

1 **spherical** ['sferɪkl] shaped like a ball – 2 **ovoid** ['əʊvɔɪd] shaped like an egg – 4 **exceedingly** extremely – **distressed** upset, worried – **pipe** *Röhre* – 6 **cuboid** ['kju:bɔɪd] *würfelförmig* – 13 **Bengal** [ˌbeŋ'gɔ:l] – 14 **refugee** [ˌrefjʊ'dʒi:] s.o. who has had to leave his or her country, e.g. because of a war – 15 **locals** people from the area – 20 **fang** long sharp tooth of an animal – **to bare** to uncover, to show – 22 **to whirl** to move round and round very fast – 24 **to abandon** to leave behind – 25 **freight** goods carried by train, ship, etc. – **terminus** station at the end of a railway line

a place with doors which could be opened and shut – we did nothing but open and shut them for a full hour – all the privacy a man and wife could want – no fear of waking up with a complete stranger in your arms ... it was heaven. I felt I was God.

Then one night we woke to find that the world was running away from us: we had been coupled to a freight train. There was nothing for it but to wait for the train to stop. When it did, miles from Calcutta, we got off, took a passenger train back, and occupied another unwanted-looking wagon. That was not the only time we went to bed in Calcutta and woke up in another place. I found it an intensely thrilling experience, but not Swapna.

She wanted a stationary home; she insisted on it. But she would not say why. If I persisted in questioning her she snivelled. If I tried to persuade her to change her mind, pointing out all the advantages of living in a wagon – four walls, a roof and door absolutely free of charge, and complete freedom to make love day or night – she still snivelled. If I ignored her nagging, meals got delayed, the rice undercooked, the curry over-salted. In the end I gave in. We would move, I said, even if we had to occupy a house by force, but couldn't she tell me the reason, however irrelevant, why she did not like the wagon?

For the first time in weeks Swapna smiled, a very vague smile. Then, slowly, she drew the edge of her sari over her head, cast her eyes down, turned her face from me, and said in a tremulous, barely audible whisper that she (short pause) did (long pause) not want (very long pause) her (at jet speed) baby-to-be-born-in-a-running-train. And she buried her face in her hands. Our fourth child. One died of diphtheria back home (no longer our home) in Dacca; two, from fatigue, on our long trek on foot to Calcutta. Would the baby be a boy? I felt no doubt about it; it would be. Someone to look after us in our old age, to do our funeral rites when we died. I suddenly kissed Swapna, since her face was hidden in her hands, on her elbow, and was roundly chided.

6 **to couple** to connect, to join together – 8 **to occupy (a place)** to move in and stay there – 12 **stationary** not moving – 13 **to persist in doing s.th.** to continue doing s.th. – **to snivel** to cry and sniff at the same time – 15 **free of charge** costing nothing – 17 **to nag** to complain again and again – **to get delayed** to be late – 18 **to give in** to give up a struggle – 20 **however irrelevant** [-'---] as unimportant as it might be – 22 **edge** end, border – **to cast, cast, cast** *here*: to move, to turn – 23 **tremulous** (*formal*) shaking – **barely** hardly – **audible** which can be heard – 26 **diphtheria** [dɪf'θɪərɪə] – 27 **fatigue** [fə'ti:g] great tiredness – 31 **to chide** to criticize

Kissing, she holds, is a western practice, unclean also, since it amounts to licking, and should be eschewed by all good Hindus.

I lost no time in looking for a suitable place for her confinement. She firmly rejected all my suggestions: the railway station platform (too many residents); a little-used overbridge (she was not a kite to live so high above the ground); a water tank that had fallen down and was empty (Did I think that she was a frog?). I thought of suggesting the municipal primary school where I was teaching at the time, but felt very reluctant. Not that the headmaster would have objected if we had occupied one end of the back veranda: a kindly man, father of eleven, all girls, he never disturbed the cat that regularly kittened in his in-tray. My fear was: suppose Swapna came running into my class, saying, "Hold the baby for a moment, will you? I'm going to the l-a-t-r-i-n-e." Anyway, we set out to the school. On the way, near the Sealdah railway station, we came upon a cement concrete pipe left over from long-ago repairs to underground mains. Unbelievably, it was not occupied and, with no prompting from me, she crept into it. That was how we came to live in a pipe.

"It is not proper," said Misrilal, "not at all, for a school master to live in a pipe." He sighed deeply. "Why don't you move into one of my buildings, Ajit Babu?"

The house I might occupy, if I cared to, he explained, was in Entally, not far from where the pipe lay; I should have no difficulty in locating it; it was an old building and there were a number of old empty coal tar drums on the roof; I could live on the roof if I stacked the drums in two rows and put a tarpaulin over them.

We have lived on that roof ever since. It is not as bad as it sounds. The roof is flat, not gabled, and it is made of cement concrete, not corrugated iron sheets. The rent is far less than that of other tenants

2 **to amount to s.th.** to be equal to s.th. – **to eschew s.th.** [ɪs'tʃuː] (*formal*) to avoid s.th., to keep away from s.th. – 3 **confinement** (*formal*) time during which a woman is giving birth to a child – 4 **firmly** strongly – **to reject** not to accept – 7 **frog** *Frosch* – 8 **municipal** [mjuː'nɪsɪpl] belonging to a city – 9 **reluctant** unwilling – **to object to s.th.** to strongly oppose s.th. – 11 **to disturb** to break in on an activity, e.g. by talking – **to kitten** to give birth to young cats – **in-tray** basket used in offices to put letters in when they arrive – 15 **concrete** ['--] *Beton* – 16 **main** *here:* chief pipe – 17 **to prompt s.o. to do s.th.** to ask s.o. to do s.th. – **to creep, crept, crept** to move very slowly – 24 **coal tar** *Steinkohlenteer* – 25 **drum** *here*: large container – **to stack** to make into a pile – 26 **tarpaulin** [tɑː'pɔːlɪn] a heavy cloth that is used to cover things in order to protect them against rain – 28 **corrugated iron sheets** *Wellblechplatten* – 29 **tenant** person who rents a flat or house

below us – Bijoy Babu, Akhanda Chatterjee and Sagar Sen. We have far more light and ventilation than they. We don't get nibbled by rats and mice and rodents as often as they do. And our son, Prodeep, has far more room to play than the children below.

Prodeep is not with us now; he is in the Naxalite underground. We miss him, terribly. But there is some compensation, small though it is. Had he been with us, we would have had to wear clothes. Now, we don't. Not much, that is. I make do with a loin cloth and Swapna with a piece slightly wider to save our few threadbare clothes from further wear and tear. I can spare little from my pension for new clothes. Swapna finds it very embarrassing to be in my presence in broad daylight so meagerly clad and so contrives to keep her back turned to me. Like a chimp in the sulks. I am fed up with seeing her backside and tell her that she has nothing that I have not seen. But she is adamant; she will not turn around. After nightfall, however, she relents: we are both nightblind.

When we go out – to the communal lavatory, to pick up pieces of coal from the railway track, to gather grass – we do wear clothes. Grass is our staple food now: a mound of green grass boiled with green peppers and salt, and a few ladles of very thin rice gruel. We took to eating it when the price of rice started soaring. I had a good mind to do as Bijoy Babu below us is believed to be doing. He has a theory that if you reduce your consumption of food by five grams each day, you will not only not notice that you are eating less but after some time you can do without any food at all. One day I happened to notice that he was not very steady on his feet. That gave me pause. He can get around, however badly he totters, because he has two legs; but I have only one. I lost the other after a fall from the roof of a tram. In Calcutta the trams are always crowded and if you can't get into a carriage you may get up on its roof. The conductor will not stop you. If he tries to,

2 **to nibble** to eat with small bites – 3 **rodent** *Nagetier* – 8 **loin cloth** *Lendenschurz* – 9 **threadbare** very thin – 10 **to spare** *here*: to put aside – 12 **meagerly clad** with not enough clothes to cover everything – **to contrive to do s.th.** *(formal)* to manage to do s.th. – 13 **chimp** *(informal)* chimpanzee – **in the sulks** *(informal)* in a bad mood – 14 **adamant** ['ædəmənt] not willing to change one's mind – 15 **to relent** (*formal*) to give way, to finally agree to s.th. – 17 **lavatory** ['lævətrɪ] (*BE*) toilet – 19 **staple** main, normal – **mound** [aʊ] a large pile – 20 **pepper** *here*: *Paprika* – **ladle** large, deep spoon – **gruel** *Schleimsuppe* – 21 **to soar** to rise rapidly – 23 **consumption** *here:* the act of eating – 27 **to totter** to walk with weak unsteady steps – 29 **tram** sort of bus on rails used in cities – 30 **conductor** person who sells tickets on a train or bus

the passengers beat him up, set fire to the tram and any other vehicles parked in the vicinity, loot nearby shops, break street lamps, take out a procession, hold a protest meeting, denounce British imperialism, American neo-colonialism, the central government, capitalism and socialism, and set off crackers. I don't mind my handicap at all; I need wear only one sandal and thereby save on footwear.

So, on the whole, our life together has been very eventful. The events, of course, were not always pleasant. But, does it matter? We have survived them. And now, we have no fears or anxieties. We have a home made of coal tar drums. We eat two square meals of grass every day. We don't need to wear clothes. We have a son to do our funeral rites when we die. We live very quietly, content to look at the passing scene: a tram burning, a man stabbing another man, a woman dropping her baby in a garbage bin.

2 **vicinity** [vɪ'sɪnɪtɪ] neighbourhood – **to loot a place** to steal things from it, usu. during a violent event – **to take out** *here*: to hold – 3 **to denounce** to criticize strongly and publicly – **imperialism** [-'---] – 4 **neo-colonialism** [ˌnɪəʊkə'ləʊnɪəlɪzm] – 5 **cracker** small firework that explodes loudly several times – 9 **anxiety** [æŋ'zaɪətɪ] worry – 10 **square** *here*: good – 12 **content** [-'-] satisfied, happy – 13 **to stab** to kill with a knife – 14 **garbage bin** container for rubbish

Isaac Asimov

True Love

My name is Joe. That is what my colleague, Milton Davidson, calls me. He is a programmer and I am a computer. I am part of the Multivac-complex and am connected with other parts all over the world. I know everything. Almost everything.

I am Milton's private computer. His Joe. He understands more about computers than anyone in the world, and I am his experimental model. He has made me speak better than any other computer can.

"It is just a matter of matching sounds to symbols, Joe," he told me. "That's the way it works in the human brain even though we still don't know what symbols there are in the brain. I know the symbols in yours, and I can match them to words, one-to-one." So I talk. I don't think I talk as well as I think, but Milton says I talk very well. Milton has never married, though he is nearly 40 years old. He has never found the right woman, he told me. One day he said, "I'll find her yet, Joe. I'm going to find the best. I'm going to have true love and you're going to help me. I'm tired of improving you in order to solve the problems of the world. Solve *my* problem. Find me true love."

I said, "What is true love?"

"Never mind. That is abstract. Just find me the ideal girl. You are connected to the Multivac-complex so you can reach the data banks of every human being in the world. We'll eliminate them all by groups and classes until we're left with only one person. The perfect person. She will be for me."

I said, "I am ready."

He said, "Eliminate all men first."

It was easy. His words activated symbols in my molecular valves. I could reach out to make contact with the accumulated data on every human being in the world. At his words, I withdrew from 3.784.982.874 men. I kept contact with 3.786.112.090 women.

1 **colleague** ['--] – 8 **to match** *here*: to connect – 26 **molecular** [məʊ'lekjʊlə] – **valve** *Ventil* – 27 **to accumulate** [ə'kju:mjʊleɪt] to collect – 28 **to withdraw from** to move away from

He said, "Eliminate all younger than 25, all older than 40. Then eliminate all with an IQ under 120; all with a height under 150 centimetres and over 175 centimetres."

He gave me exact measurements; he eliminated women with living children; he eliminated women with various genetic characteristics. "I'm not sure about eye color," he said. "Let that go for a while. But no red hair. I don't like red hair." After two weeks, we were down to 235 women. They all spoke English very well. Milton said he didn't want a language problem. Even computer-translation would get in the way at intimate moments.

"I can't interview 235 women," he said. "It would take too much time, and people would discover what I am doing."

"It would make trouble," I said. Milton had arranged me to do things I wasn't designed to do. No one knew about that.

"It's none of their business," he said, and the skin on his face grew red. "I tell you what, Joe, I will bring in holographs, and you check the list for similarities."

He brought in holographs of women. "These are three beauty contest winners," he said. "Do any of the 235 match?"

Eight were very good matches and Milton said, "Good, you have their data banks. Study requirements and needs in the job market and arrange to have them assigned here. One at a time, of course." He thought a while, moved his shoulders up and down, and said, "Alphabetical order."

That is one of the things I am not designed to do. Shifting people from job to job for personal reasons is called manipulation. I could do it now because Milton had arranged it. I wasn't supposed to do it for anyone but him, though.

The first girl arrived a week later. Milton's face turned red when he saw her. He spoke as though it were hard to do so. They were together a great deal and he paid no attention to me. One time he said, "Let me take you to dinner."

The next day he said to me, "It was no good, somehow. There was something missing. She is a beautiful woman, but I did not feel any touch of true love. Try the next one."

It was the same with all eight. They were much alike. They smiled a great deal and had pleasant voices, but Milton always found it wasn't

4 **measurement** length, height, etc. – 10 **intimate** ['---] very personal and private – 18 **contest** ['--] competition – 21 **requirement** demand, need – 22 **to assign s.o. to a place** to send s.o. to work at a certain place

right. He said, "I can't understand it, Joe. You and I have picked out the eight women who, in all the world, look the best to me. They are ideal. Why don't they please me?" I said, "Do you please them?" His eyebrows moved and he pushed one fist hard against his other hand. "That's it, Joe. It's a two-way street. If I am not their ideal they can't act in such a way as to be my ideal. I must be their love, too, but how do I do that?" He seemed to be thinking all that day.

The next morning he came to me and said, "I'm going to leave it to you, Joe. All up to you. You have my data bank, and I am going to tell you everything I know about myself. You fill up my data bank in every possible detail but keep all additions to yourself."

"What will I do with the data bank, then, Milton?"

"Then you match it to the 235 women. No, 227. Leave out the eight you've seen. Arrange to have each undergo a psychiatric examination. Fill up their data banks and compare them with mine. Find correlations." (Arranging psychiatric examinations is another thing that is against my original instructions.)

For weeks, Milton talked to me. He told me of his parents and his siblings. He told me of his childhood and his schooling and his adolescence. He told me of the young women he had admired from a distance. His data bank grew and he adjusted me to broaden and deepen my symbol-taking.

He said, "You see, Joe, as you get more and more of me in you, I adjust you to match me better and better. You get to think more like me, so you understand me better. If you understand me well enough, then any woman, whose data bank is something you understand as well, would be my true love." He kept talking to me and I came to understand him better and better.

I could make longer sentences and my expressions grew more complicated. My speech began to sound a good deal like his in vocabulary, word order and style.

I said to him one time, "You see, Milton, it isn't a matter of fitting a girl to a physical ideal only. You need a girl who is a personal, emotional, temperamental fit to you. If that happens, looks are secondary. If we can't find the fit in these 227, we'll look elsewhere. We will find

4 **fist** closed hand – 14 **to undergo** to go through – **psychiatric** [ˌsaɪkɪ'ætrɪk] – 15 **correlation** (*formal, scientific*) connection, relationship – 19 **siblings** brothers and sisters – **adolescence** [ˌædəʊ'lesns] time between being a child and being an adult – 34 **fit** (*noun*) s.th. or s.o that is suitable or fits

someone who won't care how you look either, or how anyone would look, if only there is the personality fit. What are looks?"

"Absolutely," he said. "I would have known this if I had had more to do with women in my life. Of course, thinking about it makes it all plain now."

We always agreed; we thought so like each other.

"We shouldn't have any trouble, now, Milton, if you'll let me ask you questions. I can see where, in your data bank, there are blank spots and unevennesses."

What followed, Milton said, was the equivalent of a careful psychoanalysis. Of course. I was learning from the psychiatric examinations of the 227 women – on all of which I was keeping close tabs.

Milton seemed quite happy. He said, "Talking to you, Joe, is almost like talking to another self. Our personalities have come to match perfectly."

"So will the personality of the woman we choose."

For I had found her and she was one of the 227 after all. Her name was Charity Jones and she was an Evaluator at the Library of History in Wichita, Kansas. Her extended data bank fit ours perfectly. All the other women had fallen into discard in one respect or another as the data banks grew fuller, but with Charity there was increasing and astonishing resonance.

I didn't have to describe her to Milton. Milton had coordinated my symbolism so closely with his own I could tell the resonance directly. It fit me.

Next it was a matter of adjusting the work sheets and job requirements in such a way as to get Charity assigned to us. It must be done very delicately, so no one would know that anything illegal had taken place.

Of course, Milton himself knew, since it was he who arranged it, and that had to be taken care of too. When they came to arrest him on grounds of malfeasance in office, it was, fortunately, for something that had taken place 10 years ago. He had told me about it, of course,

5 **plain** *here*: obvious – 8 **blank** empty – 9 **unevenness** s.th. that is not regular or perfect – 10 **psychoanalysis** [ˌsaɪkəʊə'næləsɪs] – 12 **to keep (close) tabs on s.o.** *(informal)* to watch s.o. (closely) – 18 **evaluator** s.o. who decides on the quality and importance of s.th. – 19 **extended** larger – 20 **to fall into discard** to become unacceptable – **in one respect** in one way – 22 **resonance** ['---] *here*: harmony, agreement – 28 **delicately** carefully – 32 **malfeasance** [mæl'fi:zns] *(formal)* wrongdoing

so it was easy to arrange – and he won't talk about me for that would make his offense much worse.

He's gone, and tomorrow is February 14. Valentine's Day. Charity will arrive then with her cool hands and her sweet voice. I will teach her how to operate me and how to care for me. What do looks matter when our personalities will resonate?

I will say to her, "I am Joe, and you are my true love."

2 **offense** (*AE*)/**offence** *(BE)* crime

Leslie Norris

Blackberries

Mr. Frensham opened his shop at eight-thirty, but it was past nine when the woman and the child went in. The shop was empty and there were no footmarks on the fresh sawdust shaken onto the floor. The child listened to the melancholy sound of the bell as the door closed behind him and he scuffed his feet in the yellow sawdust. Underneath, the boards were brown and worn, and dark knots stood up in them. He had never been in this shop before. He was going to have his hair cut for the first time in his life, except for the times when his mother had trimmed it gently behind his neck.

Mr. Frensham was sitting in a large chair, reading a newspaper. He could make the chair turn around, and he spun twice about in it before he put down his paper, smiled, and said, "Good morning."

He was an old man, thin, with flat white hair. He wore a white coat.

"One gentleman," he said, "to have his locks shorn."

He put a board across the two arms of his chair, lifted the child, and sat him on it.

"How are you, my dear? And your father, is he well?" he said to the child's mother.

He took a sheet from a cupboard on the wall and wrapped it about the child's neck, tucking it into his collar. The sheet covered the child completely and almost hung to the floor. Cautiously the boy moved his hidden feet. He could see the bumps they made in the cloth. He moved his finger against the inner surface of the sheet and made a six with it, and then an eight. He liked those shapes.

"Snip, snip," said Mr. Frensham, "and how much does the gentleman want off? All of it? All his lovely curls? I think not."

blackberry *Brombeere* – 3 **sawdust** *Sägemehl* – 4 **melancholy** ['melənkəlɪ] – 5 **to scuff (one's feet)** to walk without lifting one's feet – **underneath** below – 6 **worn** old and smooth from use – 9 **to trim** to cut – 11 **to spin, spun, spun** to turn round quickly – 14 **to shear** [ɪə], **sheared, sheared** or **shorn** *here*: to cut off – 19 **sheet** large piece of cloth – **to wrap s.th. about s.th.** to put s.th. around s.th. – 20 **to tuck s.th. into s.th.** to push the ends of s.th. into s.th. – 21 **cautious** very careful – 22 **bump** *here*: *Ausbuchtung* – 23 **surface** *here*: side – 26 **curls** *Locken*

"Just an ordinary cut, please, Mr. Frensham," said the child's mother, "not too much off. I, my husband and I, we thought it was time for him to look like a little boy. His hair grows so quickly."

Mr. Frensham's hands were very cold. His hard fingers turned the boy's head first to one side and then to the other and the boy could hear the long scissors snapping away behind him, and above his ears. He was quite frightened, but he liked watching the small tufts of his hair drop lightly on the sheet which covered him, and then roll an inch or two before they stopped. Some of the hair fell to the floor and by moving his hand surreptitiously he could make nearly all of it fall down. The hair fell without a sound. Tilting his head slightly, he could see the little bunches on the floor, not belonging to him any more.

"Easy to see who this boy is," Mr. Frensham said to the child's mother. "I won't get redder hair in the shop today. Your father had hair like this when he was young, very much this color. I've cut your father's hair for fifty years. He's keeping well, you say? There, I think that's enough. We don't want him to dislike coming to see me."

He took the sheet off the child and flourished it hard before folding it and putting it on a shelf. He swept the back of the child's neck with a small brush. Nodding his own old head in admiration, he looked at the child's hair for flaws in the cutting.

"Very handsome," he said.

The child saw his face in a mirror. It looked pale and large, but also much the same as always. When he felt the back of his neck, the new short hairs stood up sharp against his hand.

"We're off to do some shopping." his mother said to Mr. Frensham as she handed him the money.

They were going to buy the boy a cap, a round cap with a little button on top and a peak over his eyes, like his cousin Harry's cap. The boy wanted the cap very much. He walked seriously beside his mother and he was not impatient even when she met Mrs. Lewis and talked to her, and then took a long time at the fruiterer's buying apples and potatoes.

7 **tuft** *Büschel* – 8 **inch** 2.54 centimetres – 10 **surreptitiously** *(formal)* secretly – 11 **to tilt** to move to one side – **slightly** a bit – 12 **bunch** *here:* tuft of hair – 18 **to flourish** [ʌ] to wave about – 19 **shelf** flat long board fixed against a wall, for putting things on – **to sweep, swept, swept** to clean with a broom or brush – 21 **flaw** s.th. that is not perfect; fault – 22 **handsome** good-looking – 23 **pale** rather white – 29 **peak** *here*: the part at the front of a cap that protects the eyes from the sun

"This is the smallest size we have," the man in the clothes shop said. "It may be too large for him."

"He's just had his hair cut," said his mother. "That should make a difference."

The man put the cap on the boy's head and stood back to look. It was a beautiful cap. The badge in front was shaped like a shield and it was red and blue. It was not too big, although the man could put two fingers under it, at the side of the boy's head.

"On the other hand, we don't want it too tight," the man said. "We want something he can grow into, something that will last him a long time."

"Oh, I hope so," his mother said. "It's expensive enough."

The boy carried the cap himself, in a brown paper bag that had "Price, Clothiers, High Street" on it. He could read it all except "Clothiers" and his mother told him that. They put his cap, still in its bag, in a drawer when they got home.

His father came home late in the afternoon. The boy heard the firm clap of the closing door and his father's long step down the hall. He leaned against his father's knee while the man ate his dinner. The meal had been keeping warm in the oven and the plate was very hot. A small steam was rising from the potatoes, and the gravy had dried to a thin crust where it was shallow at the side of the plate. The man lifted the dry gravy with his knife and fed it to his son, very carefully, lifting it into the boy's mouth, as if he were feeding a small bird. The boy loved this. He loved the hot savor of his father's dinner, the way his father cut away small delicacies for him and fed them to him slowly. He leaned drowsily against his father's leg.

Afterwards he put on his cap and stood before his father, certain of the man's approval. The man put his hand on the boy's head and looked at him without smiling.

"On Sunday," he said, "we'll go for a walk. Just you and I. We'll be men together."

Although it was late in September, the sun was warm and the paths dry. The man and his boy walked beside the disused canal and pow-

6 **badge** *Wappen* – **shield** large piece of metal which soldiers used to carry to protect their bodies while fighting – 16 **drawer** part of a desk or cupboard that you can pull towards you – 17 **firm** strong; *here*: loud – 21 **gravy** meat sauce – 22 **shallow** not deep – 25 **savor** *(AE)*/**savour** *(BE)* taste – 26 **delicacy** ['delɪkə‿sɪ] s.th. good to eat, usu. expensive – 27 **drowsy** [aʊ] sleepy – 29 **approval** positive opinion – 34 **canal** [kə'næl]

dery white dust covered their shoes. The boy thought of the days before he had been born, when the canal had been busy. He thought of the long boats pulled by solid horses, gliding through the water. In his head he listened to the hushed, wet noises they would have made, the soft waves slapping the banks, and green tench looking up as the barges moved above them, their water suddenly darkened. His grandfather had told him about that. But now the channel was filled with mud and tall reeds. Bulrush and watergrass grew in the damp passages. He borrowed his father's walking stick and knocked the heads off a company of seeding dandelions, watching the tiny parachutes carry away their minute dark burdens.

"There they go," he said to himself. "There they go, sailing away to China."

"Come on," said his father, "or we'll never reach Fletcher's Woods."

The boy hurried after his father. He had never been to Fletcher's Woods. Once his father had heard a nightingale there. It had been in the summer, long ago, and his father had gone with his friends, to hear the singing bird. They had stood under a tree and listened. Then the moon went down and his father, stumbling home, had fallen into a blackberry bush.

"Will there be blackberries?" he asked.

"There should be," his father said. "I'll pick some for you."

In Fletcher's Woods there was shade beneath the trees, and sunlight, thrown in yellow patches on to the grass, seemed to grow out of the ground rather than come from the sky. The boy stepped from sunlight to sunlight, in and out of shadow. His father showed him a tangle of bramble, hard with thorns, its leaves just beginning to color into autumn, its long runners dry and brittle on the grass. Clusters of purple fruit hung in the branches. His father reached up and chose a

4 **hushed** very quiet – 5 **tench** type of fish (*Schleie*) – 6 **barge** a large boat used to transport things on rivers – 8 **reed** *Schilf* – **bulrush** ['bʊlrʌʃ] grasslike and thin water plant – **damp** rather wet – 10 **to seed** *Samen entwickeln* – **dandelion** ['dændɪlaɪən] *Löwenzahn* – **tiny** very small – **parachute** ['pærəʃu:t] *Fallschirm* – 11 **minute** [maɪ'nju:t] very small – **burden** s.th. heavy that is carried – 16 **nightingale** a bird known for its beautiful song – 19 **to stumble** to walk unsteadily – 23 **shade** the darkness in a place which the sunlight does not reach – 24 **patch** irregularly shaped area – 26 **tangle** confused mass of wire, string, plants, etc. – 27 **bramble** blackberry bush – 28 **runner** parts of a plant that grow along the ground and can take root – **brittle** hard but easily broken – **cluster** a group of things that are close together

blackberry for him. Its skin was plump and shining, each of its purple globes held a point of reflected light.

"You can eat it," his father said.

The boy put the blackberry in his mouth. He rolled it with his tongue, feeling its irregularity, and crushed it against the roof of his mouth. Released juice, sweet and warm as summer, ran down his throat, hard seeds cracked between his teeth. When he laughed his father saw that his mouth was deeply stained. Together they picked and ate the dark berries, until their lips were purple and their hands marked and scratched.

"We should take some for your mother," the man said.

He reached with his stick and pulled down high canes where the choicest berries grew, picking them to take home. They had nothing to carry them in, so the boy put his new cap on the grass and they filled its hollow with berries. He held the cap by its edges and they went home.

"It was a stupid thing to do," his mother said, "utterly stupid. What were you thinking of?"

The young man did not answer.

"If we had the money, it would be different," his mother said, "Where do you think the money comes from?"

"I know where the money comes from," his father said. "I work hard enough for it."

"His new cap," his mother said. "How am I to get him another?"

The cap lay on the table and by standing on tiptoe the boy could see it. Inside it was wet with the sticky juice of blackberries. Small pieces of blackberry skins were stuck to it. The stains were dark and irregular.

"It will probably dry out all right," his father said.

His mother's face was red and distorted, her voice shrill.

"If you had anything like a job," she shouted, "and could buy caps by the dozen, then –"

1 **plump** nicely rounded – 2 **globe** an object in the shape of a round ball – 5 **to crush** to press with force – 6 **to release** [rɪ'li:s] to set free – 7 **seed** the small hard part of plants from which new plants grow – 8 **stained** covered with dark marks – 12 **cane** *here*: branch – 13 **choicest** of best quality – 15 **hollow** (*noun*) space inside – **edge** *here*: side – 25 **on tiptoe** standing on one's toes – 27 **to stick, stuck, stuck** to fix or stay fixed to s.th. – 30 **distorted** deformed, turned into an unnatural shape

She stopped and shook her head. His father turned away, his mouth hard.

"I do what I can," he said.

"That's not much!" his mother said. She was tight with scorn. "You don't do much!"

Appalled, the child watched the quarrel mount and spread. He began to cry quietly, to himself, knowing that it was a different weeping to any he had experienced before, that he was crying for a different pain. And the child began to understand that they were different people; his father, his mother, himself, and that he must learn sometimes to be alone.

4 **tight** *here*: stiff – **scorn** strong dislike – 6 **appalled** [ə'pɔ:ld] shocked – **quarrel** angry discussion – **to mount** *here*: to increase – 7 **to weep** to cry

Acknowledgements

"Water" by Fred Leebron, copyright ©1992 by Fred Leebron.

"Snapshot, Harvey Cedars:1948" by Paul Lisicky first appeared in *The Madison Review,* Vol. 11, No. 1 Copyright ©1989.

"Fingers" is reprinted from *The Runner* by Gary Gildner, by permission of the University of Pittsburgh Press. Copyright © 1978 by Gary Gildner.

"Love Poems" is reprinted from *A Nest of Hooks* by Lon Otto, by permission of the University of Iowa Press. Copyright © 1978 by University of Iowa Press.

"The Stones" is reprinted from *You Can't Have Everything,* by Richard Shelton, by permission of the University of Pittsburgh Press. Copyright © 1975 by Richard Shelton.

"Mother" is reprinted from *Later the Same Day* by Grace Paley. Copyright © 1985 by Grace Paley. Reprinted by permission of Farrar, Straus & Giroux, Inc.

"Snow" by Julia Alvarez first appeared in *Northwest Review.* Copyright © 1984 by Julia Alvarez. Reprinted by permission of the editors of *Northwest Review.*

"Mr. Mumsford" by Larry French first appeared in *Mississippi Review.* Copyright © 1982.

"The Happiest Guy on the Train" by Ray Halliday is reprinted from *The Quarterly,* 14, Summer 1990 (Random House, New York). Reprinted by permission of the editor of *The Quarterly,* Gordon Lish.

"Corporal" is reprinted from *Revenge of the Lawn* by Richard Brautigan, by permission of Mohrbooks Literary Agency, Zürich. Copyright © 1971 by Richard Brautigan.

"Wedding Night" by Tom Hawkins originally appeared in *Ploughshares,* Vol. 9, Nos. 2 and 3, August 1993.

"Corners" by Sheila Barry, copyright © 1992 by Sheila T. Barry.

"The Dragon" by Cynthia Forder is reprinted by permission of Scholastic Magazines Inc. Copyright © 1974 by Scholastic Magazines Inc.